Breaking the Sound Barriers

9 DEAF SUCCESS STORIES

JULIE POSTANCE

Deaf Children
Australia

Published in Australia by
Deaf Children Australia
Street: 597 St Kilda Road, Melbourne, VIC 3004, Australia
Postal: PO Box 6466, St Kilda Road Central, Melbourne, VIC 8008
Tel: + 61 3 9539 5300
National Helpline Number: 1800 645 916
Fax: +61 3 9525 2595
TTY: +61 3 9510 7143
Email: info@deafchildrenaustralia.org.au
Website: www.deafchildrenaustralia.org.au

First published in Australia 2009
Copyright © Julie Postance 2009

National Library of Australia
Cataloguing-in-Publication entry

Author:	Postance, Julie Lynn, 1973– Breaking the sound barriers: 9 deaf success stories/Julie Postance.
Edition:	1st. ed
ISBN:	9780980595307 (pbk.)
Subjects:	Deaf children. Parents of deaf children. Deaf. Deafness. Success.

Dewey Number: 649.1512

Cover photography by Lawrence Pinder, Leader Community Newspapers
Cover layout and design by Art Attack
Printed in Australia by Griffin Press
Typeset in Caslon 224 Book 10.5pt on 15pt

Disclaimer
All care has been taken in the preparation of the information herein, but no responsibility can be accepted by the publisher or author for any damages resulting from the misinterpretation of this work. All contact details given in this book were current at the time of publication, but are subject to change.

The stories in the book are based on the experience and opinions of the contributors. They do not reflect the views of the author or of Deaf Children Australia.

The advice given in this book is based on the experiences of the individuals. Professionals should be consulted for individual problems. The author and publisher shall not be responsible for any person with regard to any loss or damage caused directly or indirectly by the information in this book.

Deaf Children Australia has been enriching the lives of deaf and hard of hearing children, young adults and their families for 149 years.

Acknowledgments

I WOULD LIKE TO ACKNOWLEDGE the thousands of children and adults with hearing loss and their families for the diversity, joy, courage and greatness that they bring to the world.

I would like to thank all the people who contributed their stories: Sofya Gollan, Joanna Fricot, David Brady, Chevoy Sweeney, Olivia Andersen née Gemmell, Roz Keenan, Gavin and Rebekah Rose-Mundy, Gail Smith and Lizzie Eakin. Without their willingness to examine their own lives to help others, this book would not have been possible.

I am grateful to Deaf Children Australia for publishing this book and providing the support to make this book a reality. In particular, I would like to thank Damian Lacey, Veronica Pardo and my colleagues at Deaf Children Australia.

I extend my thanks and appreciation to Dorothy O'Brien, author of *The Cochlear Implant: Parents tell their story* for sharing her knowledge and experience.

Thanks also to volunteers Katie Jenner, Katy McKay and Gloria Calescu for transcribing the interviews, to Melita Granger and Helen Farrell for editing the manuscript and to Gillian Postance for proofreading the manuscript. Last, but not least, I would like to thank my partner, Wes, for his love and support during the development of these pages.

BREAKING THE SOUND BARRIERS

Contents

Foreword

FOR THOSE INTERESTED IN THE THEMES that resonate in the lives of deaf people, there is a wealth of information to be found. Books, journals, online and video resources abound that tell the story of the challenges that deaf people experience.

What is more difficult to find are the stories of deaf and hard of hearing people themselves. These stories also abound, but they are obscured in the recesses of oral histories, stories that are told and retold within the community of people who are deaf and hard of hearing, but rarely find their way to the printed page.

In *Breaking the Sound Barriers*, nine inspirational stories have been brought to light. They serve to educate, in the way only storytelling can do, about the struggles, joys, challenges and potential that deaf people experience in their lives.

Whether it is gaining access to a quality education, or finding opportunities to engage in community life, deaf people often struggle to enjoy the benefits that hearing people take for granted. If you venture into this world, you will know that struggle is the frequent precursor to amazing success, for it is only when we are challenged that we discover our innate capacity to fight injustice and succeed despite the odds.

Parents of deaf children are frequently inundated with messages about the difficulties they will encounter. Their own limited experience of deafness may result in fears about the future. Our aim in publishing this collection is to tear down the myth that deaf people cannot achieve their potential. While we acknowledge the reality that life as a deaf person brings many unique challenges, some of which can be construed as barriers, they need not shape the whole life experience of deaf people. The life experiences of deaf people bring a rich and diverse perspective, one that enriches our cultural and linguistic identity.

We would like to thank all the participants who shared their stories for this book. Their 'voices' are an essential part of our mission, which is to promote liveability and life abilities for deaf and hard of hearing Australians. We also extend our deep appreciation to Julie Postance whose vision and dedication to this project has created a unique and wonderful resource for families. Together, Julie and the nine storytellers have provided a genuine interpretation to our vision: A life to be lived – deaf people empowered, connected and achieving.

Damian Lacey
CEO
Deaf Children Australia, Deaf Services Queensland and
WA Deaf Society

Introduction

HAS YOUR CHILD JUST BEEN DIAGNOSED with hearing loss? Have you been experiencing the effects of hearing loss on your child and your family for several years? Then this book is for you.

Breaking the Sound Barriers came about as a result of the calls that thousands of parents of newly diagnosed deaf and hard of hearing children make to Deaf Children Australia's national Helpline each year.

Many parents report experiencing shock, grief, confusion and worry about what lies ahead after the diagnosis. Many complain that at once, all the hopes and dreams they have held for that child disappear. The most commonly asked questions to the Helpline staff are: 'My child is deaf. Will they lead a normal life?', 'Will my child ever drive?', 'Will they get married?', 'Will they find a job?' 'Will they be happy?' 'Will they be successful?'

The answer to all of these is a giant resounding YES! Far from being a disability, deafness merely sets a child on a different journey, certainly not a lesser one. Having worked in the Media and Public Relations Department at Deaf Children Australia, I have enjoyed the privilege of listening to and writing about countless stories about deaf and hard of hearing children who, despite various barriers, are enjoying active, full, happy and successful lives just like children with normal hearing. Thanks to the love and support of their families and organisations such as Deaf Children Australia, these kids are realising their full potential every single day.

I have also had the honour of speaking with deaf and hard of hearing adults who have undergone challenge after challenge in the hearing world, yet have gone on to become highly successful CEOs and managers of organisations, businessmen and women, film directors, sportspeople, wives, husbands, mothers and friends.

The need became increasingly apparent on my behalf to share these inspiring stories so that you too could benefit from them and incorporate some of the winning strategies they have used into your own lives if you so chose.

Breaking the Sound Barriers is not about hiding from the realities of living with deafness in a hearing oriented world. In this collection of nine stories, five parents of deaf and hard of hearing children paint a very candid portrayal of the challenges, struggles and barriers that their families have come up against in raising a deaf child and the strategies they have used to deal with them.

Some contributors speak of the lack of available information and support with deafness and their ignorance about where to turn to for support. Some report being propelled into a strange highly politicised world of deafness where different organisations appear to push different agendas.

Others tell of infuriating experiences with deafness professionals and education authorities. Others report being discouraged by some proponents of auditory verbal methods from using Auslan – the sign language of the Australian Deaf community.

Others have taken heat from the Deaf community for using hearing aids or cochlear implants. These are the experiences of some of the parents in these pages. This book does not in any way attempt to censor those.

The stories in this book provide many insights, learnings, tools and strategies in dealing with hearing loss. Who better to offer these to you than parents of deaf children who have overcome many obstacles to give their child the best future, alongside inspirational deaf adults who have been through it all before?

You will read about how Joanna Fricot's initial feelings of isolation led her to speak to another parent who had gone through a similar experience. It was the motivation she needed to create her own support group and write her own booklet for parents of deaf children.

You will obtain an insight into how Roz Keenan succeeded in implementing Auslan as the second language taught at the mainstream school attended by her deaf daughter, Sarah; and how Gail Smith's six-year legal battle revolutionised deaf education in Queensland.

A parent's initial reactions to their child's deafness is one thing, but what about their ongoing association with it? Chevoy Sweeney shares how her open acceptance of her son's deafness taught him not only to feel comfortable in his own skin, but also to equate deafness with perfection.

Deafness is often spoken about as 'the invisible disability', and the stark absence of strong deaf voices – whether they be signed, spoken or written – is often lamented. It was with great pleasure, therefore, to be able to provide through this book, the strong voices of five extraordinary deaf role models, who share in their own words, exactly what it is like to be deaf.

Indeed, no book about deaf children would be complete without their authentic perspectives as they explore their journeys with deafness, the challenges they have faced and the tools they have used to navigate successfully through life in a hearing world.

You will read how David Brady dealt with issues of social isolation – what it was like being the only one in his school who was deaf – and how despite numerous setbacks, he succeeded in becoming the national business operations manager of Touch Football Australia, representing Australia in the 2005 Deaflympic Games in water polo, and climbing three of Britain's highest mountains in less than 24 hours.

Sofya Gollan shares with you how despite her nightmarish high school years, she has gone on to become a respected actor, director of award winning feature films, a sign language presenter on the children's TV program, *Play School*, and a much loved wife and mother.

Profoundly deaf Olivia Andersen née Gemmell explains her feeling of being in-between worlds – neither hearing nor signing – and how her experiences only succeeded in making her a stronger, more determined woman. You will read how she went on to obtain her degree in Design, work for *marie claire* magazine, backpack through Africa, win a Winston Churchill Fellowship, become the director of her own mentoring organisation for deaf children, and marry the man of her dreams.

These generous contributors share with you their battles and victories, obstacles and opportunities, pressures and lessons. They reveal the skills they have developed to compensate for a lack of hearing, the mindset they needed to cultivate to cope and flourish, and the beliefs they have had to nurture when barriers have sometimes seemed insurmountable.

There is no one way to successfully raise a deaf child. *Breaking the Sound Barriers* attempts to represent a broad range of families and deaf role models from oral, signing and bilingual backgrounds, each of whom share markedly different stories and who employ vastly different strategies.

Nowhere is this more clearly seen than in Gavin Mundy's story. Gavin – a proudly deaf father of four children also with hearing loss – adopts diverse methods to raise each of his children. This includes making the controversial decision to have his daughter implanted, despite being aware of the criticism he would draw from the Deaf community, of which he is a prominent member.

In reading these stories, it is hoped you will reflect upon your own family situations and take away with you practical solutions to help you enrich your deaf child's life. Whether you do or not, the book's greatest purpose is to inspire you, to help you as a hearing parent to feel less alone. Above all, it is to make you aware that deaf people can BE, DO and HAVE anything they want in this world!

This is a book about survival, faith, courage and perseverance. A combination of these can conquer even the direst of circumstances. It is a celebration of deafness in the face of difficulty and at times, seeming impossibility.

The book does not have to be read in one sitting. You may wish to read one story at a time, learn from it and then walk away with renewed hope and a fresh perspective, before returning to the next.

With the aim of being inclusive of all kinds of deafness, I invited stories representing a range of perspectives from signing oral and bilingual backgrounds. The stories contained in this book are from participants who agreed to contribute; they are not representative of all deaf experiences. The stories were shaped from interviews, phone calls, emails and media articles. Every effort has been made to adhere as closely as possible to the contributors' voices. All contributors had the opportunity to amend and approve the final draft.

This book does not push any particular political barrow nor is it academic. I have left that role to the academics and experts in the field of deafness. As the author, I have merely been a vehicle for the contributors so that they could tell you their inspirational stories.

While *Breaking the Sound Barriers* was originally written for parents and families of deaf or hard of hearing children, it is also valuable for deaf and hard of hearing teenagers, deaf and hard of hearing adults, and professionals interested in deaf perspectives. Schools and universities will also find it a useful resource for subjects dealing with deafness.

In Australia, approximately 500 babies are born deaf each year and there are approximately 16,000 deaf children under 21. About 3.5 million Australians have hearing loss.

If you are blessed to have a child who is deaf or hard of hearing, I wish you a wonderful, fun-filled life with your child and hope that you may gain many valuable insights from reading this book.

To order a copy of this book, please call
Deaf Children Australia on 1800 645 916
or go to www.deafchildrenaustralia.org.au.
There is an order form at the back of this book.

No limitations... only the ones you consent to

Sofya Gollan, a profoundly deaf actor, writer and director, is best known for her role on *Play School* as a guest presenter who uses sign language. After graduating from the National Institute of Dramatic Art (Acting) and the Australian Film, Television and Radio School (Master of Arts Directing), Sofya spent four years with the Australian Theatre of the Deaf. Since then she has directed a one-hour telemovie and 11 short films (three of which have received awards). She has also written three feature films, which have been screened widely through Europe, the US and UK. She lives in Sydney with her husband, sculptor Robert Hawkins, and her three-year-old son Vincent.

I AM NO STRANGER TO BARRIERS. Much of my life has been about overcoming them and about fighting to get out of the box in which many have tried to place me. However, through my deafness, I have learned enormous strength, courage and determination, which has allowed me to work my way up from actor to producer and film director, and now mother and wife. Through my experiences, I have come to know that many of our limitations in life are the ones we allow people to impose on us, and that sometimes you have to set the precedent on your own, to achieve things that many would say are impossible.

The way I view my deafness can undoubtedly be attributed to the way my parents reacted to my 'gift', as they called it. Having suspected that I might be mentally delayed, the diagnosis of deafness confirmed by the sixth doctor when I was two and a half, turned out to be an enormous relief.

Back in the 70s, it was common for deaf children to be institutionalised, but my mother wouldn't hear of it and immediately set about assimilating me into the hearing world. This entailed my being fitted with the most powerful hearing aids at the time and spending more than my fair share of hours at speech therapy sessions.

I had a magical childhood. Despite being the only deaf child in a family of three sisters, I never recall feeling different from anyone around me. Rather, my memories are full of days riding ponies, gymnastic competitions, athletics training and reading books which no doubt led to my becoming a writer and director. It wasn't until I hit the later primary school years that my difference really started making itself felt. Within the family home, it was just something that we all adapted to and felt almost 'normal'.

Some of you may think that as a successful actor, writer and film director, I must have been good at school. In fact, quite the opposite is true. I had a terrible time. My struggles began in late primary school when I began to have trouble picking up what was going on in class, particularly with subjects requiring avid listening and understanding. In the end, my grades were so low, I had to repeat the whole year of Grade 6.

High school was a nightmare from day one. I found it difficult to hear anything and always sat up the front so I could concentrate. My teachers tried to assist by giving me additional material but nothing replaced that 'on the spot' class learning that gives meaning to textbook reading. So much of my energy was taken up simply trying to keep up, much less attempting to do well.

Most of the time I hid behind a mask of pretending to know what I was doing and I became an expert at covering up my comprehension gaps. This left me feeling unsure of my ability to contribute to what was going on around me. I often opted to become a watcher rather than a participator because I would make fewer mistakes that way.

Being the only deaf person at school didn't help. My situation was compounded by the fact that my parents who were both freelance journalists and novelists would move around the country, following the trail of jobs. As a deaf teenager struggling academically and socially, I certainly wasn't complaining. The minute my parents said, 'Kids, we're moving,' I felt a colossal surge of relief. It meant that I never really had to face being the lonely person in the school and the change of scenery meant I could pretend that things would change.

So many upheavals, combined with my increasing inability to access the curriculum, began to take their toll. All through my childhood I'd had dreams of becoming a doctor, but these faded with the gradual realisation that I was never going to get access to the education I needed. What was most discouraging was that no one in the school environment thought it was a profession I could aspire to. If I'd had someone who had thought a bit outside the square and encouraged me to lift my grades then I might have persevered.

By the time I was 14, I had turned into a stubborn, angry teenager, seeking refuge in the wrong crowd at an already rough school, united by our common lack of direction and loss of faith in the education system.

While my parents were always supportive and never said that there was anything I couldn't do (within reason – a career in radio was never going to be wise!), I always had the sense that they had no idea what kind of access to assistance was available. They were well aware though that I was experiencing multiple difficulties in the school system.

They decided to move back to Sydney and enrol me into a different high school, which turned me around a little. Even so, by Year 11, I was skipping two days out of five. After scraping through with below average marks in Year 10, I grew increasingly anxious about my situation, knowing the unlikelihood of ever passing Year 12.

Back then I had a real sense that I didn't measure up. I often felt unhappy and very alone. But I was also ruthlessly stubborn and very determined and I refused to be a victim. Thanks to a wonderful textiles teacher who encouraged me to follow a creative path in fashion, I began finding solace in sewing clothes and selling them to neighbours and friends. Before long, my hobby had turned into a thriving little business and my parents discussed the possibility of pulling me out of school to do an apprenticeship in fashion design at TAFE.

But life had other plans. At 16 years old, I did a two-week acting course over the school holidays with the Australian Theatre of the Deaf (ATOD). I'd always loved the idea of being an actor, but had never seen or heard of a deaf person on stage or film, so it was always a pipe dream. Now, all of a sudden, it was real. I could become a professional actor if I wanted to!

The ATOD were looking for actors and agreed that they would take me on as a trainee actor for six months if my mum and dad would support me. Thereafter, they would offer me a paid full-time job. I was over the moon.

My parents were hardly thrilled. 'Your talent is in fashion, Sofya,' Mum tried to tell me. 'At TAFE you can learn a trade and be a fashion designer.' Mum and Dad were successful writers who were able to make a living from their creative endeavours but there were many actor friends in their circle who lived from feast to famine. Understandably they worried about my fate.

However it was too late. I'd already made up my mind.

On the first day of Year 12, I turned my back on school and began my training as an actor. It was a defining point in my life. Up until now, I'd been the only deaf person in my hearing community. Now the door opened to reveal a whole new world of the deaf and its rich culture and I no longer felt so alone.

For the first time, I was surrounded by Deaf role models – some who spoke, some who didn't, all of whom used sign language – who were adamant about the fact that they were normal people with normal aspirations. Up until then, I'd felt much like a second-class citizen. Now I realised that my future started with me.

In addition to that, I was introduced to sign language and realised how much easier communication became with it and what a struggle life had been without it. I became fluent very fast and my self confidence grew.

For the next four years, I became totally immersed in the Deaf community. With hindsight, I realise that I was simply doing what many deaf young people do when, for the first time, they discover the Deaf community: that growing sense of not feeling part of the hearing world and an overwhelming urge to cut ties with the hearing world in order to slip into the comfort of being surrounded by people exactly like you.

After five years this began to wear thin as I became tired of the boxes in which I saw deaf people being placed. At that time, I felt there lacked a sense that deaf people could do anything. Instead what I observed was hearing people 'helping' deaf people, and deaf people either being placed into poorly paid, mundane jobs or being encouraged to take on community welfare positions to help others with disabilities. None of these options appealed.

I began thinking about leaving the Theatre of the Deaf and entering the mainstream world where I could make a greater impact. My sights were set on studying at Australia's National Institute of Dramatic Art (NIDA), but with 1200 hopefuls auditioning for just a handful of places, this was going to be tough.

One woman had a profound effect on me in terms of teaching me to become a self-actualised and self-driven deaf person. Carol-Lee Aquiline, an incredibly strong, culturally Deaf fellow actor from America, kept saying to me, 'Sofya, just go for it! Don't worry about people who say that you can't. Just try it and see what happens!' While others were saying, 'It's really hard out there,' she would ask, 'How are you going to make this happen?' I began to believe that the sky was the limit for me in terms of what I could achieve.

The only way I was going to get into NIDA I decided, was that I was going to have to let them know who I was! So for a whole year prior to auditioning, I made contact with the NIDA tutors, telling them how keen I was to study at NIDA.

My perseverance must have paid off because by the time the auditions came around, the examiners knew who I was.

Dislabelled Duo – Australian Theatre of the Deaf

Child of Courage – NIDA

After the gruelling audition schedule I found myself part of the final 20 people who were offered a place.

My two years at NIDA were, for the most part, a wonderful time in my life. I loved walking in the doors of NIDA each morning and gaining a world-class training alongside my classmates, Cate Blanchett, Lucy Bell, Sacha Horler and Essie Davis. Many of these classmates are still close friends.

With voice training five days a week, my voice articulation improved and my professional acting and communication skills flourished. Some of my fellow actors commented on my heightened visual acuity, my perceptiveness of human nature and my ability to inspire people. For the first time in my life, I made true friends who were hearing and I began to see myself on an equal footing.

NIDA did not have an equal access policy for people with disabilities. So when I was unable to get funding for an interpreter, I spent my inheritance on one. Back then, there was no real assistance for interpreters for individuals going through specialised institutions. So I was faced with either leaving the course or spending the money and completing my studies. That probably remains one of my biggest frustrations, that I didn't use my inheritance as a mode of financial security for the future.

After graduating in 1992, I was surprisingly one of the few graduates who got acting jobs almost immediately, working for a new company called the Australian People's Theatre, a branch of the Sydney Theatre Company with John Howard as Artistic Director. I have to confess, like all actors, I felt a bit smug that I got employment so quickly. And like all actors, unemployment came as a nasty shock when the company disbanded after three years.

For a whole year I attended audition after audition with no success. I'd become an actor because I wanted to be in films. But no one was giving me work because I was deaf and my voice was different.

When a fax came in from the National Theatre of the Deaf in New York offering a job, I jumped at it. From 1994 to 1995, I lived in Manhattan and experienced first-hand the American deaf way of life. The US is 20 years ahead of Australia in terms of their attitudes towards deaf people, their strong deaf role models and the availability of jobs for the deaf.

I saw Gallaudet University and the Rochester Institute of Technology where deaf people were achieving tertiary qualifications in whatever disciplines they dreamed of. This was in stark contrast to Australia with its lack of access to studies through interpreters and notetakers at that time.

I began to realise what was possible.

Having always dreamed of making a short film, a part of me kept saying, 'Deaf people don't direct films!' Although I'd never articulated it to myself, it was a profound sense of 'I wouldn't be allowed to tell people what to do on a film set!'

I decided to use the money I had saved from my job on a three-month intensive film-making course in New York.

As soon as the course began, I thought, 'This is a piece of cake! I can do this and so can anyone else!' My focus began to shift away from acting and on to film directing as my future.

In 1996, I came back from a year in vibrant Manhattan to house-sit my parent's house in the sleepy seaside town of Wombarra, on the southern coast of Sydney in the middle of winter. It was a massive culture shock and it took a while to find my equilibrium again.

Yet I have never allowed myself to wallow for too long and I point-blank refused to sink into creative anonymity. I began to regard this period of isolation as an opportunity to reflect on my future as a director – something which I felt increasingly drawn to do.

I began writing and producing short films, which I entered into many film festivals, most of which were screened. While making these, I applied for a directing course at the Australian Film, Television and Radio School (AFTRS) to gain more knowledge of my craft. As for many other filmmakers, it took three applications over three years before I finally got into the course. It wasn't plain sailing in that I had to prove to them that I was capable of leading films into production.

Most people make four or five films before they launch into producing a full feature film. I didn't want to risk rejection because of my deafness, so I made 10. Two of them, *Not the Usual Victim* and *Swallowing* were finalists in the 1996 and 1998 Tropfest. *Chlorine Dreams*, a film shot entirely underwater, screened all over the world. *Dressing Dad* received the ATOM award for the Best Short Documentary in 2000.

My first feature film, *Preservation*, was a gothic melodrama about a single woman, Daphne, running a taxidermy business in Sydney in the 1890s. Starring Jacqueline McKenzie, Jack Finsterer and Simon Burke, not only was it a giant leap in terms of my career because I managed to secure funding for it when the Australian film industry was at an all time low, but it was

*Directing
Jacqueline
McKenzie on
the set of*
Preservation,
2003

the first time I got paid a proper salary as a director. When my movie premiered at the Sydney Film Festival in 2003 and at the 2003 Melbourne International Festival as well as being nominated for three AFI awards, I finally felt that I was getting the recognition I had so long struggled for.

My second feature, *MELT* – a drama about three girls falling for an ice sculptor passing through their country town – was picked for the highly esteemed Aurora Workshop, an exciting initiative to support Australian scripts to a higher level.

In 2006, I wrote and directed a play, *The Cat Lady of Bexley,* for the Australian Theatre of the Deaf. Performed in English and Auslan, the play juxtaposes the story of Patricia Carlon, an introverted crime writer and her experience growing up profoundly deaf in the 1940s – with a modern woman, Billie, who is battling the frustrations of living with her own late onset deafness.

I took on the role of Carlon because I knew the justice I could do to her character. Obviously my life has been very different to Carlon's who kept her deafness a secret and depended solely upon letters for communication. Unlike Carlon, I have had the benefit of hearing aids, mobile phones, the Internet and, two years ago, a cochlear implant which has made a huge difference to my life. However, it is her sense of loneliness, of being different to others, with which I can relate.

I believe, and have often been told by those with whom I work, that my deafness has brought several advantages to my career as a director. Firstly, my work is highly visual and, with film being a visual medium, this is a valuable asset. Being deaf, I've been able to sense visual cues that hearing people often miss. This has made me an excellent judge of body language and I can read faces very well. The actors I direct have not been able to get away with using their voice to cover up what they are actually revealing through their body language. I also have an innate ability to visualise and have an acute sense of what will work in the final cut.

I am well known for my role as a sign language presenter on ABC's *Play School* with which I have been involved for the past 12 years. Many tell me, and I can proudly say, that I have become

Directing Jack Finsterer on the set of Preservation, *2003*

11

a positive role model to deaf and hard of hearing children and adults. Part of being on a national program like *Play School* is the opportunity to raise awareness about deafness and sign language in a very positive way.

I live in Sydney with my partner of seven years and our little boy, Vincent, who has just turned three. Even though Vincent is hearing, we are teaching him some signs (and teaching my husband too since he has normal hearing and has been a bit lazy with picking up sign language). Life on the whole is very good, but I know that my success is directly linked to how hard I have persevered.

My advice to hearing parents of deaf and hard of hearing children would be the following: Kids should be given access to both signing and oral language because the ability to lipread relies on the extent of their vocabulary. If their vocabulary is limited, then so will be their ability to lipread. Even if your child has a cochlear implant, sign language should still be used as a back up, because there is still about 20% of the day when your child cannot use their implant – when they go to bed, when they have a bath, when they go swimming and when they are sick. During those times, sign language will aid them in still feeling like part of the family. Sign language will also help your child communicate with other deaf people who may not have implants. It still remains an important consideration for identification with the deaf world – which *will* happen at some point in their life.

There is a lot of value for kids with multiple disabilities being in specialist schools because of the resources available, which might not be available in regular schools. However, if your child is simply deaf and is able to get access to teachers of the deaf, interpreters and notetakers in a mainstream school, then I believe there is more value in them being integrated into the wider community. This is also important for the wider community to see deaf people as an integral, valuable (and non-scary) part of society.

Deaf children are never going to be able to avoid isolation completely because deafness *is* an isolating disability. Inclusion is based on language and how well your child can communicate with another. As a parent, you need to provide support for your child, let them feel that they can express what is going on for them and that you value their point of view.

The reality is that the high school years are going to be tough because high school is all about fitting in and belonging. There will be times when the other kids won't want to be seen with someone who is that little bit different. However, you can assure them it does get better, the older they get. If they get to 16 or 17 and have even a couple of good friends, then they will be ahead. The older they get and the more autonomous they become, the more skills they will develop to carve a life in the real world and the happier they will be.

One of the hardest things to learn (well, for me it was) is that it's okay to ask for help and that it doesn't make you 'more disabled'. It took me a long time to realise that most people just want to help if they can. If you can be open to that, then you will find there are resources you can seek out to make life easier. I think it's about creating community, accomplishing through many people what is very difficult to do alone.

That has been my aim these last few years, trying to find out what my community is and what it is I need in order to live a successful life. I know I don't belong within the deaf world, but I'm not 100% accepted in the hearing community either – especially in my life's work. So my task has been to find out who my friends are and maintain those relationships, regardless of hearing ability.

I am at the stage in my career where I want to make more progress with making films in the wider community. Using my expertise and understanding of sign language in the community I have just made a DVD resource called *SignBaby*, for those who want to teach their child to sign whether they are deaf or hearing.

One of the amazing things for me recently is to discover how much easier life is with the cochlear implant. I resisted having it for a long time thinking that it would not give me enough benefit to make the surgery worthwhile, but I have been very fortunate that my 'hearing' took to it.

Having said that, it's not the cure to all of my communication problems. I still don't talk on the phone (I'm still too scared to try!) and need to teach myself how to do that. The funny thing is that I now see how 'easy' life is when you can hear enough. I speak from a perspective of a lifetime of struggling to communicate well so what I can hear now might be terrible for another person with an implant after a lifetime of hearing.

It's all relative. That's what I used to tell myself when I was really upset and frustrated as a teenager: that I didn't have a monopoly on misery, that others may not be deaf but might have completely different challenges. That used to make me feel much better. I know it's perverse but knowing you're not in it alone does help you lift yourself up.

Being deaf is part of me. It has shaped my life in profound ways, sometimes for the better. Looking for the positives in every situation will take you a lot further than if you dwell on the negatives.

I am proof of that.

Breaking the invisible glass between us

Joanna Fricot is mother to nine-year-old Estelle, who is severely deaf. Estelle mainly uses oral language to communicate, attends a mainstream school with her hearing brothers, and plans to run her own hairdressing salon one day. Joanna is the creator of the Parents of the South East Region support group in Melbourne, aimed at parents of deaf and hard of hearing children. She is also the brainchild of the support booklet, *Where Do We Go From Hear?* – a collection of stories written by parents of deaf children.

NO ONE CAN PREPARE YOU for when you first hear the news your child is deaf. I remember the moment like it was yesterday. I can still see the audiologist – her cherry red shirt and trendy thick black-framed glasses, looming over us, test results in hand.

'Your daughter is severely deaf,' she said coldly.

I felt a slab of concrete cement my heart.

'My daughter is deaf...,' I repeated slowly.

'Yes, and it is permanent.'

Tears rolled down my husband Albert's cheeks while I held our 22-month-old daughter tightly on my lap. 'She has never heard us say "I love you",' I whispered. We sat in stunned silence. Then my tears joined Albert's.

In the haze that was the next few hours, the trendy lady spoke coolly about 'next steps' but I couldn't take in a word. Inside I raged, desperately wanting her to go away so that I could pretend this wasn't happening to our family. I hated how she'd stripped away any hope for my daughter's future – such was my ignorance of deafness at that time – and replaced it with a show bag full of medical mumbo-jumbo and a new child I wasn't sure I could raise.

I'd always known that something was different about Estelle. Having often been unwell with infections, I'd been continually anxious about the baby's health. I hadn't enjoyed the pregnancy as I had my first two. When Estelle was born by caesarean on 30 July 1999, I'd felt strange, unsure.

'I'm worried that something's wrong with Estelle,' I had told the nurse, but she'd assured me that I was suffering from the 'third day blues' and had given me a sleeping tablet. The niggling feeling in my gut remained, however, and simply wouldn't let me rest.

The day I brought Estelle home from the hospital, I whispered into her tiny ears, 'Welcome to your new home. I love you.' Little did I know she couldn't hear me. Over the next few months, I sang her songs, but she didn't respond to them in the same way her two older brothers had. Nor did she react to sounds and games, like when we played peek-a-boo or hide-n-seek. Instead, she became frightened and would burst into tears when you jumped out from behind the door.

I found it difficult to connect with her in the way I had with the boys. It felt like there was an invisible glass between us. I hated

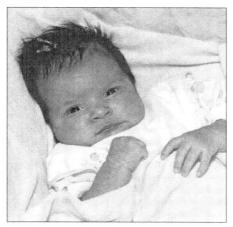

Estelle, four weeks old

this feeling. I was stricken with guilt and desperate for answers. When I mentioned this to the doctors, they labelled it 'sleep deprivation'. Yet two visits to sleep clinics did nothing to resolve the problem. *She had passed hearing tests conducted by my health nurse, our local GP and an ENT specialist so why was I so worried?* they said. I knew that she was only passing the tests because she was responding to the movements she was seeing. My family began to question my health and all of a sudden, it became my issue, not Estelle's.

With no speech at 14 months, not even 'mama' or 'dada', she was developing far slower than her peers. She became frustrated when other kids came to visit and began to smack her brothers when they talked to her.

Tired of receiving no reaction from doctors, I decided to take on the role of doctor myself. Placing ear plugs in my ears one day, all of a sudden, the source of all Estelle's angry frustration became blazingly obvious. I began to get down on the ground at her level to play. I stopped calling out her name from a distance, made sure that she could always see my face and lips, used lots of facial expressions and played the *Wiggles* video really loud. And then it was like magic. I had a much happier child. The invisible glass between us began to collapse. My suspicions about her deafness were confirmed.

Again, I begged doctors to test her hearing, but my requests fell flat. Instead, we were referred to a paediatrician who

17

diagnosed her with a behavioural problem. I steadfastly refused to accept this.

Finally, at the age of 22 months, after carting Estelle from one specialist to another, we found one who permitted her to be tested by an audiologist. And then there it was. At last, she was confirmed deaf.

As soon as she was diagnosed, the shock and relief were huge. Shock, because I knew almost nothing about deafness (there was no family history and I didn't know anyone who was deaf) and I prayed that it was only grommets. And relief, because they had finally confirmed what I had suspected since she was six months old, despite no one believing me. With my severely limited knowledge of deafness, I assumed that treatment would fix whatever Estelle had. How naïve my thinking was...

For the first few weeks, the grief was immense. My deceased grandmother had always told me, 'Jo, cry hard when you receive bad news because this is how you will make way for tears of joy.' So that is what I did. I cried and cried on our bed for days and nights, repeatedly asking myself what I'd done wrong for this to happen to us. Most of all, I cried from the guilt, always my greatest hurdle. Guilt that for so many months, my baby hadn't heard my (nor any one else's) voice; that she'd been submerged in soundless loneliness.

With each cry, I became tougher and the grief gradually transformed to relief and determination. It was time, I decided, to make up for all the lost time with my daughter. It was time this invisible glass came down, once and for all. Now that we'd identified the issue, I had a ton of work to do, not the least of which was changing my parenting methods and learning new skills.

The 'show bag' full of detailed brochures on hearing aids, hearing equipment and early intervention centres presented to me at Estelle's diagnosis did nothing to alleviate my anxiety. In fact, its sombre medical contents only served to bewilder me further until I was reduced to a blubbering wreck.

All I wanted to do was to speak to another mum who had experience in raising a deaf child. I craved to hear her tell me with confidence that everything would be okay. But I could find no parenting booklets nor contact details of other parents of deaf children and there was no one in my family or community who was deaf.

I called one of the early intervention centres begging them to put me in touch with a mother of a deaf child of primary school age. Several weeks later, I was given the name and number of a mother in Brighton whom I contacted immediately.

Speaking to her was the tonic I needed. She gave me hope and made me see that all the dreams she'd initially had for her daughter were still achievable, regardless of her hearing loss. I still regard her as my angel of hope. I could see the light after that which created the first step to regaining my confidence in parenting.

Since that call, I have been able to accept Estelle's disability. I focus instead on finding the gifts in having a child with hearing loss. And indeed, in searching for those gifts, I have found them. I was able to begin working on our bond which has since become as strong as even the most tightly-knit mother-daughter relationship. Every day, I remind myself that all I want for my daughter is for her to meet her highest destiny. All we have is this lifetime to make that all possible.

So desperate were we to make up for lost time that we did whatever it took to help Estelle communicate. On her second birthday she was fitted with hearing aids. While we sang 'Happy Birthday' to her, her big brown eyes grew wide in amazement at the first sounds of our voices. Then, in a tiny voice, she sang back, 'I bid day'!

She is a candidate for a cochlear implant, but there's a chance she could lose what little hearing she has. So we have left the decision in her hands for when she's older. Right now, she's doing really well with her hearing aids.

At any rate, she could make some sounds so, with speech therapy and home practice, we worked on those so that they gradually became words. We learned everything we could about the hard of hearing world and its role in today's society. Our family learned to sign because we were told that Estelle may not be oral. But we always spoke to her while signing, leaving the choice in her hands as to how she preferred to communicate.

Having her two older brothers to play with helped her interaction no end, but she clearly needed to socialise with other children of her own age. From the age of three, we sent her four days a week to a bilingual program at an early intervention centre for the deaf in Burwood. To see her little legs board a bus at 7.30am, her tiny frame weighed down by a backpack far larger than she was, would bring tears to my eyes. It also – surprise, surprise – elicited a mountain of guilt. But if our little girl was ever going to catch up with her peers, this was absolutely fundamental. It certainly paid off – for everyday we noticed she had more and more language.

Gradually she dropped her signing and became increasingly oral. 'I like talking because sign language is hard and my hands get tired,' she told me. 'I keep forgetting the signs, but I never forget the words!'

In order to spend as much time with her as I could, I volunteered my time at the school as a creative dance instructor. This provided me with the opportunity to regularly observe how she interacted with her teachers and peers and identify what needed reinforcing at home. It also allowed me to witness her strengths and achievements which helped lessen the guilt and intensify my pride.

Having a deaf child, you are always recommended so many different methods by so many different experts. Despite holding a huge respect for them, I have never let them nor others dictate to me about what they think is best for my child. It is vital not to doubt one's own instinct. After all we, as parents, know our children and their capabilities best.

When Estelle was five, we faced the agonising decision of whether to keep her at the early intervention school for the deaf or place her in mainstream education. In her two and a half years at the deaf school, she had done so well and was so content and comfortable there. But it had always been our vision to see her attend the mainstream school with her brothers. It was time to test not only whether she could cope in the hearing world, but also how the hearing world would cope with her.

I had no illusions about how tough it was going to be for her. When she began Prep at the local Catholic school, I had to brace myself for her deluge of questions that would come once her classmates began interrogating her about her deafness.

'Mum, why am I the only one wearing hearing aids in the family?' she asked me one day. I knew that this question would eventually crop up, but I never knew quite how I was going to answer it. Without thinking, I found myself looking at her class photo.

'Do all the kids in your class look and sound the same?' I asked.

'No,' she replied unhesitatingly.

'See. Every one of you is different. Look – different hair, different eyes, different sizes, different colours of skin. Each one of you is different and this is what makes you all special.'

She seemed to accept it for a moment, then asked, 'But why my hearing?'

I should have known. She was such a bright little thing and couldn't help always being one step ahead of me. I took a deep breath and silently prayed for help.

'Pregnancy is like opening a Christmas gift from God or Santa. All year you look forward to Christmas day because you know you will open up a gift that will be special. It may not be exactly what you wanted, but then that gift finds a special place in your life and becomes part of who you are. Your hearing loss is what makes you, Estelle. You were my gift to unwrap and discover.' I do not know where my answer came from, but it seemed to work because she smiled and changed the subject.

There have been times, however, when she has walked through the door and the look on her face has broken my heart. Her biggest challenge has not been inside the classroom, but in the social interaction outside it. She is unable to hear what the kids are saying in the playground when several are speaking at the same time, or when they are speaking some distance away from her. Sometimes they'll say things like, 'Estelle, you can't play this game because you can't hear us.' Kids will be kids and I've had to teach her to stand up for herself.

Estelle was given a baby doll for her birthday and I noticed to my surprise that she'd used a black marker to draw two hearing aids on the doll's ears. Most kids would have drawn make up, but she clearly needed the doll to resemble her. I asked her why she'd done this.

'This is my baby,' she replied earnestly. 'And babies look like their mums.'

I was amazed.

I decided to spend the afternoon making hearing aids moulds for the doll, which she then proudly took to her 'show and tell' at playgroup. While all the hearing kids gathered around intrigued, we introduced her deaf baby and answered their questions about its deafness.

There surely couldn't have been a more wonderful way to educate her classmates and increase their awareness about her aids being an integral part of her life. The doll was then happily placed in the play corner so that each time someone dressed the doll, its aids would go on. It made Estelle feel accepted and confident enough to wear them not only at the deaf school but at the mainstream one too.

Each of these steps helped Estelle's transition into the world of the hearing. It also assisted me as her mother to know that her self-esteem around accepting her hearing loss was growing.

As a parent you try to do your best to teach life skills but having a child with a hearing loss has only made me more determined to do my best. Sometimes I want to protect Estelle from the pain that goes with not hearing, but the reality is: she is who she is. I can't protect her from that. The sooner I accepted her hearing loss then the better it would be for her to cope and understand herself in this hearing world.

We've even had situations where parents have told their kids not to play with Estelle because 'she might not be able to understand'. It is sad that people generally don't know how to react to deafness, but I believe it's up to parents of deaf children to educate them. You simply have to go out there and tell people to speak directly to your child's face, slow down and be clear. Then it's fine.

Despite the hardship, we know that placing Estelle in a mainstream school has been the right thing for her. We've been fortunate that her school has been so supportive of her needs. Along with a visiting teacher twice a week, she receives a teacher's aide and specialised equipment, including a soundproofed classroom. All of her teachers are accepting and approachable and wear RF units which transmit their voice directly to Estelle's hearing aids.

She is now in Grade 3, has learned to hold her own with her hearing peers, is confident, happy, and has loads of friends.

Estelle takes part in a 'dance off for deaf kids' with Demi Sorono from So You Think You Can Dance. *From left to right: Lucas Smyrnis, Estelle Fricot and Demi Sorono*

At nine, she loves to learn and has dreams to own her own hairdressing salon. The sky is the limit for her. When Estelle was younger, she was convinced that when she grew up she would no longer need her hearing aids. But now she accepts that they are part of who she is. She is who she is and she is proud of that.

I have had to teach my family to adapt to Estelle's needs. At home, Albert and I don't treat her any differently to her brothers. At the dining table we always make every effort to ensure she is heard and will often stop the conversation to make sure this happens. This is not always easy to do as I never want to spoil Estelle or mislead her into thinking she is always going to get our (or anyone else's) special attention.

During family discussions we consulted Estelle about what would best suit her communication needs. In the early days we used her RF unit at home, but it gradually became redundant. Estelle's brothers have learned to speak in plain view of her where she can see their lips. We eliminate background noise so she can clearly hear them. Our house has floorboards so that she can hear the vibrations of noise and music.

The boys have become skilled at including Estelle in their discussions, at repeating questions without getting annoyed and not simply assuming she has heard or understood. More and more we have become aware that spending quiet time with her without having any disruptions in the background greatly enhances her wellbeing.

My own initial feelings of isolation and desperate need for support made me think about all the other families out there who must feel similarly when their children are diagnosed. This led me to start up the Parents of the South East Region (POSER) group in Melbourne in November 2004 with the help of Deaf Children Australia. Now with around 25 members, this

Estelle with AFL star, Jason Akermanis, at the launch of the Where Do We Go From Hear? *booklet on 10 July 2007*

group has a primary aim of providing friendship, inspiration and support to families of deaf and hard of hearing children in Victoria's south-eastern suburbs. It now meets regularly to swap ideas about parenting strategies.

My goal has always been to replace the 'show bag' with a booklet containing real life stories of parents with deaf children and of the deaf children themselves. I wanted others in the same situation to have access to their contact details so that they would have the chance to get in touch with them. In July 2007, together with guidance and funding from Deaf Children Australia, the *Where Do We Go From Hear?* booklet was launched and is now available nationwide.

Since its launch, many families of newly diagnosed deaf children have told me that the booklet has given them hope and brought them answers.

In the last few years, I have given many interviews and shared my story with many magazines, newspapers, radio stations and TV programs. While at times, I have been criticised for my willingness to appear in the public eye, I believe this is crucial if we want to better educate the hearing public about the best ways to interact with deaf people. As a parent of a deaf child, I see it as my natural duty to promote more understanding and awareness of deafness out in the community. Who else is going to do it if we don't?

If testing had been compulsory (or if the health professionals had listened to a mother's instinct), Estelle would have been diagnosed at three months old. The fact is, testing is still not enforced in every state – just with babies who are premature and/or with a history of hearing loss. A child who is diagnosed before they are six months old still has the chance, with speech therapy, to have normal speech.

Joanna with Estelle at the launch of the Where Do We Go From Hear? *booklet on 10 July 2007* Photo: Paul Loughnan, Stonnington Leader

Estelle's speech is very good purely because I interacted with her as though she were deaf, way before her official diagnosis. Please, if you suspect your child is deaf, never take no for an answer. Persistence is the key. Never, never, never give up!

Parenting a child with hearing loss was a journey I never thought I would have to undertake. But it came into my life in a bundle wrapped in pink. Since travelling this road of deafness with my daughter, I have always been grateful for the love and support of my husband, Albert, my boys, Adam and Shaun, my extended family and my friends.

'Despite never having attended university, Estelle has been my degree. Through her, I have learned about patience and resilience, tolerance and perseverance.'

I have also sought and relied upon the support of Deaf Children Australia and the support of my local community. I hope Estelle will one day stand proud knowing that she has never journeyed alone.

Despite never having attended university, Estelle has been my degree. Through her, I have learned about patience and resilience, tolerance and perseverance. Together we have attained so many things I never thought were possible. She has been a deep joy in my life. I am so grateful to God that He brought her to me.

3

Deafness is not in the ear; it is in the mind

David Brady is the national business operations manager of Touch Football Australia. A graduate of University of New South Wales in Social Sciences, with a Masters Degree in Sports Management from the University of Sheffield in the UK, David has also represented Australia at the 2005 Deaflympic Games in water polo and has climbed three of Britain's highest mountains in 24 hours. In his spare time, he mentors deaf and hard of hearing youth and their parents in Sydney and Melbourne. He currently lives in Canberra and communicates using both oral and sign language.

I SEE LIFE AS A HUGE CHALLENGE. There is nothing I love more than embarking on new adventures and showing others that being deaf really doesn't hold you back. It is simply about finding a way to achieve whatever it is you want in life.

Deaf academy award-winning actress, Marlee Matlin, once said, 'The handicap of deafness is not in the ear; it is in the mind. The only thing I can't do is hear.' These words have become the mantra by which I live.

I am not saying that it has been easy to live with deafness. Like anyone, I have had my fair share of setbacks and obstacles that life tends to throw at you – setbacks and obstacles which only seem to multiply when you are perceived by others to have a 'disability'. But I have always held fast to the belief that life is not what happens to you. It is how you react to it and I have learned to adjust the way I respond to those obstacles until I get the outcomes I want.

I believe that it is due to this ability to remain positive and enthusiastic, despite the world often appearing an unsupportive and brutal place, that I have come to be National Manager of a sporting association, to represent Australia in the 2005 Deaflympic Games in water polo and to climb three of Britain's highest mountains in less than 24 hours.

Like most of you reading this book, I was not born with a silver spoon in my mouth. My family did not have the benefit of newborn hearing screening that is available today. The diagnosis of 'profoundly deaf' when I was two years old would have come as a colossal shock to my hearing parents, considering that I was their first child, there was no history of deafness in the family and they had virtually no background knowledge on the subject. My deafness was caused by a rubella epidemic contracted by my mother during pregnancy. Add to that the difficulty of living in the sleepy 20,000-strong rural town of Armidale, northern New South Wales, where there were no other deaf kids in my age group and virtually no specialist support.

I was fortunate, however, to have been born to parents with a survival attitude, which I believe was instrumental in shaping my own 'can do' attitude. If my parents had ever experienced the typical roller coaster of emotions of denial, grief and shock associated with hearing parents discovering that their child is deaf, they certainly never made me aware of it. Instead they had me fitted with – what were then the latest, but what would now be considered – clunky, old-fashioned, box-type hearing aids and made the best of the situation as they could.

Alongside speech therapy, Mum set about teaching me to lipread and speak as many words as I could absorb so that I would not fall behind my age group. While sign language was an option, there was little point learning it, with so few deaf people in my town.

'A is for apple, B is for bear, C is for cat,' she would chant endlessly, hour upon hour, pointing at each letter of the alphabet on the vibrantly coloured animal poster pinned to our living room wall. I would sit there patiently, repeating the words the way I would see and hear them until she would smile with approval and move onto the next one. She was determined that I learn to speak perfectly and without a hint of an 'accent'.

At the same time, she threw herself into tracking down other families of deaf and hard of hearing children and began her own support group. The purpose was to connect our family with others who were in the same boat as well as to expose me to other deaf kids. The group must have done a lot for Mum and Dad because it became a major part of our lives. The shared dinner parties,

Me at 11 years old with my brother Jeff and sister Sam

ten pin bowling afternoons and group holidays became the fabric of my childhood.

Mum also encouraged my younger brother Jeff and my sister Sam to support me. From early on, they became my greatest helpers, quietly whispering in my ear if I didn't hear a conversation clearly and keeping me posted on what was happening on TV. Their thoughtfulness was, and is to this day, a source of great comfort.

With no other alternatives in Armidale, my parents sent me to a regular pre-school where I was the only child who was deaf. I can honestly say that I failed to notice that I was different to any of the other children in the class. I merely thought that they were all deaf like I was!

When it came time to send me to primary school, my parents were faced with one of many decisions that have to be made when you have a deaf child: whether to send me away to a specialist school in Sydney or keep me at home in Armidale where I'd attend the mainstream school and receive support from the town's local deaf unit. For them, the choice was simple: at the local school I could keep interacting with the 'real world' and stay at home and close to the family. So that is what I did.

Being the only deaf child in my class at Armidale Primary, my classmates would sometimes pick on me, or I'd find myself getting left behind in class because I was unable to follow what was going on. But as far as I was concerned, life was far too much fun to care! I believed that school was for playing, not learning. I would play games with whoever wanted to play them with me and my passion for sport, my highly competitive nature and my tendency to win at anything physical guaranteed me no shortage of friends.

From early on, sport became my language. Who needs spoken communication when you could throw yourself into the universally recognised rules of hockey, rugby and soccer? My parents, delighted that I had found something that connected me with hearing kids, encouraged this passion as much as they could. My years at the school were some of the happiest of my life.

But things took a turn for the worse as soon as I reached high school. I'd had one teacher for the whole of the school year in primary school; now I had one teacher for *each* subject. Comprehending anything in class was often infuriatingly difficult. Mum would do the best she could and advocate for my needs in the classroom, and the specialist teacher (one of only two specialist teachers in the whole of the north-west region of NSW at that time) tried hard with me, but it was still a struggle.

Social interaction became my biggest hurdle. Many of the kids with whom I'd attended primary school moved away to different high schools and those remaining who'd been my friends during the carefree days of primary school without warning became distant. Suddenly it desperately mattered to them who they hung out with and with whom they were seen. Most broke off into their own little groups, none to which I belonged. While the girls never failed to be polite towards me, 'hearing impaired' simply didn't quite cut it at the time.

I recall one particularly hurtful experience when I discovered that one of the cute girls liked me. I was on my way to speak to her when I lipread her friend whispering in her ear, 'Be careful, he's deaf. He'll be too much trouble for you.' It was one of the most devastating moments of my teenage years.

How do you stand a chance when you are regarded as even slightly different from a group of adolescents, all of whom are striving to be the same? Adolescence was one of the roughest periods in my life, but I now realise how much it shaped my resilience for the future.

There were times when I wanted to become a recluse and retreat from the world, but I simply couldn't bring myself to do that. As far as I was concerned, once people stepped on to the sports field, we were all equal. Sport had taught me to *participate* and strive to win. It helped me prove myself in the hearing world.

'Right!' I thought adamantly, 'If I can't win socially, I'll win on the sports field!' And that's exactly what I did. Where sport had always been my passion, it now became my obsession, my outlet, my escape from what was going on at school. While most of my classmates were 'hanging out', I threw myself into hockey, swimming, athletics. It really didn't matter. All I knew was that I wanted to be the best I could at all of them.

At times, attaining this was a bitter struggle. During the zone trials, many selectors refused to pick me for the team because of my 'disability', despite them knowing full well that I was the best player. Rather than let this deter me however, I simply tried and retried until they'd accept me for the team.

Once, I recall, during the 50 metre backstroke, I failed to hear the gun go off and came last. My swim coach, concerned about this sudden downturn of fortune, negotiated with the swim officials that for the next race – the 50 metre breaststroke – I would stand in lane two – the closest lane to the starter gun – so that I could see its smoke coming from it when it was fired. Fuelled by anger from losing the previous race, I swam better than I'd ever done and not only won it, but also took out the interschool final. I was stoked! From then on, I always chose lane two, despite lane five being offered to the fastest qualifiers and I always finished first, despite not being able to hear the starter gun. I bet you didn't know that smoke appears from the starter gun before the sound does...

Gradually, my persistence began to pay off and I became the school champion in virtually every sport. First, it was swimming and one of my highlights was winning the 100 metre breaststroke at the interschool swimming competition. When the crowds roared, the buzz I felt to be competing against other schools and knowing that I was part of a team was one of the most exhilarating feelings I had ever experienced. If I had one piece of advice to deaf kids, it would be to find something you are passionate about, something you love doing, preferably where you can be part of a team. It will get you through the bad times and keep your self-worth high.

'If I had one piece of advice to deaf kids, it would be to find something you are passionate about – something you love doing – preferably where you can be part of a team. It will get you through the bad times and keep your self-worth high.'

The philosophy of persistence which I applied to sport, I also applied to my school work. I knew that I needed to be extra focussed on my studies and work longer and harder hours than my hearing classmates if I was going to keep ahead of the game. There were times in class, particularly group discussions, when I'd find it virtually impossible to follow what was going on. But I persevered and simply did whatever it took to succeed.

There were times when it became all too much and I would catch myself thinking, 'Why is life so hard? I wish I wasn't deaf! I wonder what life would have been like had I not been deaf?'

My mother and father, to whom I attribute a great deal of credit for who I am today, would remind me of other kids my own age who were undergoing treatment for cancer or other extreme hardships.

When I thought about these kids, it was easy to get over any of my own self-pity. 'I'm actually lucky!' I would say to myself. 'Life could be a whole lot tougher than this.' Then I'd think about all the things I could be grateful for – my health, my family, my ability to play sport and to do well at school and immediately I'd feel better.

In Year 10, Mum got a teaching post in England for a year so our family relocated to Kent where I spent the year at Longfield High. It was astounding how differently the kids there treated me in contrast to the arctic treatment I had become so used to at Armidale High. It didn't hurt, I'm sure, that I was an Aussie and good at sport, but my Longfield schoolmates were a damn sight more open-minded and respectful towards me than the Armidale kids had ever been and included me in everything they did. My guess is that living in a population of 50 million, the Brits' regular exposure to diverse cultures, races, classes and types of people would almost certainly have aided their broadened level of tolerance. Whatever the cause, I welcomed it wholeheartedly.

While in England, I travelled around Europe, experiencing for the first time the beauty and diversity of its places and cultures. More and more I became conscious of the vast world beyond the narrow confines of conservative Armidale and could no longer see any limits in terms of what I could achieve in my future. I felt confident, free and more contented than I had in years.

In 1989 I returned to Australia, to the same school, the same students and their same attitudes – a different person. I felt like

On top of Scarfel Pike, England, 24 hours Three Peaks Challenge, 1997

I'd been through a metamorphosis and had emerged a stronger, more determined person – more convinced than ever of my own capabilities. This seemed to conflict directly with some of my Armidale teachers and classmates who appeared shocked to even see me show up for the first day of Year 11. In their experience, I suppose, deaf kids never made it beyond Year 10, mostly dropping out on account of the increase in oral communication in Years 11 and 12. That was never going to be me! I'd already made up my mind that I was going to university so that I could later be a sports manager.

'What are you doing here, David?' some of the students asked me on my first day back.

'I'm back to do Year 11 just like you are!' I replied with defiance.

They looked gobsmacked. It only made me more steadfast to prove them all wrong...

For the next two years, I worked like a dog, determined not only to get my HSC, but also to qualify for university. While I was bitterly disappointed not to have had a girlfriend at that time, looking back I don't think I would have passed my HSC with that kind of distraction. Instead, I hit the books with a vengeance, studying day after day, hour after hour, mostly on my own.

By then, teachers had started wearing FM units and I would sit at the back of the classroom, the kid with the headset, feeling much like a movie star. One of my teachers, Mr Hattie, a loud genial man, would often disappear from the classroom still wearing his unit and then while speaking to another student or teacher in the corridor, would say loudly into his microphone: 'David, if you're still listening to this, switch it off now!' It would always make me grin.

Year 12 was one of the toughest years of my life. It was not only writing in structured sentences which I found gruelling. It was more so the fact that I was the only deaf student undertaking Year 12 in the whole of the west region. Despite having a principal who was very supportive of deaf education, there remained widespread ignorance about deafness and severely limited accommodation of its needs. I was determined to shatter prevailing misconceptions about deaf people not being able to undertake further study just because of their inability to hear.

I was entitled to special consideration in my exams for being deaf, which included a separate exam room, extra reading time and the use of a thesaurus or dictionary. Nevertheless this caused no end of controversy among some of my fellow students who thought that it was downright unfair. Many expressed their disapproval to teachers and some even staged mini-protests. While the sensitive part of me felt guilty, the logical side screamed, 'Stop! For once, life's rules have been slanted in my favour. I'd be a fool not to take advantage of this!'

Once again, it was hard work and sheer persistence that paid off. In 1990, as well as obtaining excellent results for HSC, I became the first deaf pupil to complete high school in my region. I received an award for my achievements and was accepted into the University of New South Wales to study Social Sciences. There is no greater sense of satisfaction than when people expect you not to achieve something and you prove them all wrong. My advice to deaf kids? Never, never, never give up! If you have big plans for your future, do whatever it takes to achieve them, regardless of what people tell you. Put your head down and work as hard as you can.

'My advice to deaf kids?
Never, never, never give up!
If you have big plans for your future,
do whatever it takes to achieve them,
regardless of what people tell you.
Put your head down and work
as hard as you can.'

My life was never the same after that. I left the town of Armidale and moved to Sydney, where I lived at a college on campus. All of a sudden, the lid on my world opened up. I loved the diversity of the uni students who, unlike high school, accepted each other for who they were. People showed interest in, rather than seemed uncomfortable with, my deafness. My social life blossomed for the first time since England. I began to make friends, real friends with whom I remain close to this day. For the first time in my life, I began to have girlfriends.

I played all kinds of sport, got involved in college activities, community days and fundraising events and applied to work on the committee. While I was never elected as a committee member, my peers voted me Collegian of the Year for my 'contribution to residential college activities and all round general enthusiasm'. It made me realise that regardless of whether you get knocked back for things, you will often be recognised for your willingness to jump into life and participate. My advice to deaf kids is get involved in everything you can. Put your hand up for things. Don't just stand on the sidelines. Get involved! Participate in life and you will begin to feel part of things.

At university, writing essays remained a challenge, but there were a great deal more resources which had not been available to me at high school. Resources included fantastic notetakers (when you could find them as they were in such short supply), support groups and lecturers who freely used an FM set so I could hear them in the vast space of the lecture theatres. I got through the lectures and tutorials by many hours of reading, plus a good memory which served me well in exams.

One of the most exhilarating moments of my life was graduating from the University of New South Wales, after three long years, with my Bachelor of Social Science degree. It was of no consequence to me not to be present for the actual ceremony. I was in London at the time where I remained for the

'When something isn't working in my life,
I have always searched for the alternative.'

next five years. What mattered most was that I'd made it this far and could now look forward to my next dream, a postgraduate degree in Sports Management.

When something isn't working in my life, I have always searched for the alternative. As soon as I began battling London's merciless employment climate, it became clear that finding a job in the traditional manner – the CV, the interview and then the long wait for a job – was simply not going to bring me any joy. Yet I was determined that I wasn't going to end up on the unemployment scrap heap. So when the twelfth rejection letter came hurtling through my letterbox, I didn't become bitter or resentful. I simply put on my best Marks and Sparks suit and went door knocking!

There were times when I couldn't get past the curt words of the cranky receptionist at the front desk. But it was those other occasions when the managers agreed to meet me, that I

'Don't wait for people to come to you because you could wait forever. Go to them and demonstrate that you are capable of doing anything.'

realised I was taking a fundamental role in changing my future. Once they met me face to face and realised just how serious I was about the job and that I could do it just as well as any other applicant, more often than not I walked out of the office with a triumphant grin.

Over the next few years, I worked as a front of house footman for a five-star hotel in Clifton where I got to meet famous people including the Queen Mother! I worked as a bar manager in a noisy nightclub, did data entry for the British Government Tax Office, and later became a payroll professional in corporate London. The money I made paid for my travels through Russia and Scandinavia. What did I learn? Don't wait for people to come to you because you could wait forever. Go to them and demonstrate that you are capable of doing anything.

At the time, I was coaching hockey and playing in the British National League – the highest league you could play. But it wasn't enough. I wanted more! I wanted to be the CEO of a sports organisation. So at 25, after saving every penny I had, I enrolled into the University of Sheffield to do my Masters Degree in Sports Management. While I knew that writing a thesis would be hard, I was willing to pay that price.

And, was it a price! I found it extremely difficult, and at times near on impossible. It wasn't so much coming up with ideas that was the difficult part. It was writing well-worded essays which was a constant source of frustration. Add to that the fact that I was no longer receiving assistance from a notetaker or any of the other resources I had received at NSW University. Yet giving up was not an option. I knew that if I was to function in the real world, I was going to have to learn how to write with no mistakes. I was also determined to do better than I'd done in my first degree. So I began asking friends for help and employed an English grammar tutor to assist me with my writing. I did whatever it took to succeed.

Proudly holding my Masters Degree, Graduation, Sheffield 1998

Two and a half years later, I had completed a 20,000 word thesis on disabilities in sport and had my Masters Degree in

Sports Management. The day of my graduation was one of the most thrilling days of my life. Seeing my parents' faces flushed with emotion as I received the blue and gold rolled up certificate from the university's vice chancellor, made all the challenges, frustrations, arduous work and late nights worth it. That day reinforced my belief that there is no limit to what you can do and where you can go in life.

Life has a habit of throwing us curve balls. When I returned to Australia in 1999, I received a rude awakening. Naïvely assuming that my high level of qualifications and UK employment experience would stand me in good stead for a job of some stature, this illusion died as soon as I began receiving the rejection letters.

It took 70 applications, 40 interviews and 12 months of frustration to secure my first job. I will never forget the despair of trying to convince potential employers during interviews that my hearing impairment would not be a major hurdle. Sometimes I wonder what kept me going during that difficult year. I guess it was my fighting spirit which always begged me never to give up.

During that time, I called upon every strategy I could think of to help me succeed. I decided to treat getting a job like playing in a sports match and the only way to win the game was to practise it until I was perfect. I got experts to scrutinise and perfect my CV. I did mock interviews with friends and family members, refining my answers to tough interview questions, repeating them over and over until they became second nature. I met with anyone in the sporting industry who agreed to meet me so that I could glean any tips about getting my foot in the door. I did whatever it took to win.

Then one meeting changed my luck forever. A friend of my father's put me in touch with an Ann Mitchell, the CEO of Sydney

University Women's Sports Association and Greg Harris, CEO of Sydney University Sports Union, who both kindly agreed to meet me to talk about the industry. After showering me with all manner of advice and contacts, Ann Mitchell called a week later to offer me a part-time role as sports development officer at the Association. I was over the moon!

Within a month, the job became full-time and I stayed there for two years. But I knew I was capable of more. In 2001, after studying part-time at the University of New England, I obtained my Graduate Certificate in Project Management which helped secure me a job as the assistant sports development manager with Sydney University Sport from 2001–2005. Following that, I became the Victorian marketing and sales manager for Dartfish, a company that develops performance-enhancing sport video training applications and exclusive televised broadcast footage. My role involved presenting to and building one-on-one relationships with a wide variety of stakeholders.

After deciding that I had enough qualifications and experience to move on from Dartfish, I experienced another seven months of job interviews, application rejections and difficulty facing interview panels who were not convinced that a deaf person could be suitable for the position in their company. It was gruelling, but I would not be beaten.

I worked at gyms, coached sports at schools, secured meetings with leading sportsmen and when I became desperate, even began looking for work outside the sports industry. But once again, persistence paid off.

On my 70th interview I hit the jackpot, securing a job as state manager for the Victorian branch of Touch Football Australia. During what was to be one of the toughest interviews I have ever had to undergo, a three-man panel fired a barrage of questions all related to whether or not I was truly capable of doing the job.

When asked if my deafness would require any extra assistance, I replied, 'There are many resources available to overcome any challenges associated with my deafness. It is also a real opportunity for staff to learn to work effectively together.'

Within a short space of time, I'd been promoted to national business operations manager of Touch Football Australia, a job to which I have always aspired. My role involves managing the business side of the sport – including finance, operating systems, membership management, marketing, and working with the association's members, sponsors and volunteers. I currently oversee six full-time and two casual staff – the first time I have ever managed people.

The job certainly has its challenges, the greatest one being to prove to the whole organisation – all 300,000 of them – that I am capable of performing this role effectively. There will always be perceptions about working with a deaf person, but I work hard to break down the barriers of fear and ignorance. I quickly let people know that I am deaf and that the best way to communicate with me is either face to face or via email.

I continue to find phone calls and conferencing a hurdle, but do my best to get the main gist of what people are saying by picking up key words and using guesswork. For example, if my colleague says, 'I sent you the document on youth administration today', I hear 'sent', 'document' and 'administration' and deduce the meaning from those words. I count myself lucky that with a volume phone and hearing loop, I am now able to use a phone. In the 80s and 90s before volume phones, I did not have this benefit. I also find it difficult at meetings, trying to lipread and write notes at the same time and colleagues do not always appreciate having to share their notes with me. Like I did with studying and applying for jobs I have learned to treat work as

Training for the Deaflympics, Noosa 2004

a game. Learning the rules helps keep you in the competition. Simple as that.

My ultimate goal is to be the CEO of a sports organisation. I believe I am halfway there. In the meantime, I continue to push my own boundaries at every opportunity. In 2005, I represented Australia in water polo at the Deaflympic Games. I play high level hockey and water polo in open competition and coach people in these as well as soccer, rugby and handball. I also coach deaf teenagers in water polo and touch football. At the moment, I'm giving Australian Rules football a go and salsa dancing – which has opened doors to a new group of people and endless laughs.

I still face daily challenges. As a capable deaf person, at times people mistakenly believe that because I can speak so well, I can hear well too. At times, people think I am ignoring them when I don't respond. I often get left out of group conversations and every day I come face to face with people who are either too scared to speak to me or simply can't be bothered repeating information when I haven't heard them. I deal with the broad misconception that hearing aids are like bionic ears, rather than what they really are: amplifiers sitting on a pair of ear lobes! For all their 140 decibels of power, they are still machines, which break down. Once I take them out, I can't hear anything at all.

When the hearing world is saving for a deposit on a house, I – like every other deaf person over the age of 21 – must save to buy new batteries for my hearing aids or the latest technology to keep up with the demands of today. Unlike in the UK, where hearing aids can be claimed on tax or repaired at the Acoustic Laboratories at no cost, deaf Australians have to fork out between $6000 and $10,000 of their own money every three years.

No, life isn't fair sometimes. But I've had to develop the attitude: 'That's the way life is. Those are the rules. That is the playing field of life. If you want to survive, if you wish to succeed, you have to learn to play by them. Or you will be left behind.'

I have learned, and am still learning, to ask for what I need. I now ask my employers for new hearing aid batteries when I require them. To date, none of them has ever said no. I have learned to read body language and lipread so well that at work conferences, I can tell what the opposition is saying on the other side of the boardroom! Through my experience with deafness, I have learned to be resilient and to never take no for an answer. I now mentor deaf teenagers and their families in Melbourne and Sydney through the mentoring organisation, *Hear For You*. I provide them with tips and guidance on possible career choices, share advice and pass on valuable lessons I have learned along the way.

My advice to parents of deaf and hard of hearing children is: 'Tell your child that they can do, be or have whatever they want in life. Never tell them that they can't do anything and encourage them never to buy into others' limitations being imposed on them. Ask them to seek help wherever possible. Find out their dreams and goals, then encourage them to work hard at those until they reach them. Never dictate to your child whether to use oral or sign as a communication method. Provide them with access to both. Your child is an individual; it should be up to them as to how they wish to get their message across.'

Sign language is an important mechanism for people unable to hear their own voice and for conversing in noisy environments. Communicating orally is much harder work and cuts off your child's valuable connection with other deaf and hard of hearing people. Despite not learning sign language when I was a child, I learned it when I came back from overseas so that I could communicate with my friends who use Auslan. I have come to value it highly as a language. Not only do I use it when I am around my deaf and hard of hearing mates, it has also been invaluable when playing water polo at the Australian Deaf Games and at the Deaflympics. There would have been no other way to communicate with my deaf team mates and deaf contestants from around the globe.

I attribute most of my success to my family (both immediate and extended) whose love and encouragement never ceases to amaze me. I am also grateful to my teachers, employers, friends and mentors who have provided advice, encouragement and guidance throughout my life. Their contribution has made my life the success it is today.

4

He's perfect!

Chevoy Sweeney is mother to eight-year-old Jarrod Brown, severely deaf. Jarrod uses sign language to communicate, attends the bilingual Thomas Pattison School for deaf and hard of hearing children and has plans to be a famous AFL player one day. Chevoy works as a professional freelance Auslan interpreter. Jarrod lives with Chevoy and his stepfather Sean, his sister Alexia, stepsister Tamar and stepbrother Oren in Seven Hills, New South Wales.

I REMEMBER IT AS CLEAR AS DAY – the moment my son Jarrod, a blonde-haired, cute little boy of four, came up to me and signed, 'I can't talk. Everyone else can, but I can't.'

It was the moment in Jarrod's life when he realised that he was different. The defining moment when he was going to have to accept who he was. It was also the moment I knew that my answer could either make or break his belief about himself.

Jarrod was born in 1996 in Nambour, Queensland. I'd had a terrible pregnancy with nausea and vomiting, all day, every day, for the whole nine months. Apart from the bump on my stomach, I was thin and gaunt. In the back of my mind, I worried that this little baby inside of me would be very sickly after it was born.

After all, how could it possibly get any nutrients from me when I'd been so ill?

After diagnoses of glandular fever, then chronic fatigue syndrome and cytomegalovirus (CMV), to my surprise, Jarrod came into this world, two and a half weeks late, weighing 10 lb 6 oz – not bad at all! So relieved was I to see a healthy baby with 10 fingers and 10 toes that all my worries faded.

But when he was about four months old, I began to grow anxious that he had a hearing impairment. Looking back, I don't remember exactly what it was that concerned me. It must have been that, at times, he wasn't turning to noise. On mentioning it to my husband and family, however, they didn't share the same concerns. Even when I told the community nurse at a check up, she assured me that I had nothing to worry about; that I was overreacting.

Over the next month, I conducted my own experiments and became further convinced that something was amiss. When I expressed my fear to my GP, he smiled and told me that nothing was wrong.

Again, I persisted with my own tests, one of which really sticks in my mind. I'd just come home from shopping one day with Jarrod asleep in the back of the car. Scooping him into my arms, I carried him into the house and lay him down on the rug in the lounge room still asleep. Then getting a saucepan and lid from the kitchen, I walked back out towards him and began banging them together, quietly at first, getting louder and louder, while at the same time, moving closer and closer towards him.

He didn't wake up. He didn't even flinch. If any of you have seen the movie *Mr Holland's Opus*, it was just like that gut-wrenching scene where the mother and her baby are spectators at a parade. While the band marches past, its trumpets, cymbals and a big bass drum noisily crashing, her sleeping baby doesn't so much as bat an eyelid. Yes... it was one of those moments.

At that time, 1996, the hearing impairment screening program wasn't available for babies. So taking things into my own hands, I called one of the hospitals in Brisbane. An appointment was made when Jarrod was six months old to have an Auditory Brainstem Response test which would assess the brain reactions to sound.

It was during this test that I found out my baby son was profoundly deaf. All of a sudden, my life became a time of utter turmoil; there were numerous visits to doctors, grieving, having to still be a mother to Jarrod's older sister and needing to make a choice about how to raise Jarrod.

Ironically enough, before having children, I'd worked as an Auslan interpreter. My interest was originally sparked from the deaf neighbours I'd had while growing up. This I'd done in a casual capacity for the four years prior to having Jarrod. So I knew how to sign, I had many deaf friends and I was aware of the Deaf community. In view of all of that, my biggest question was: *did I want Jarrod to be a part of this or did I want something different for him?*

Many have commented that it must have been so much easier for me – and in some practical ways it was. The reality was I grieved in the same way most other hearing parents of a newly diagnosed deaf child do. I had absolutely no inkling that I would have a deaf child so I grieved for all the things I didn't know, the things that made it difficult to deal with.

There was pressure on us to make a decision *there and then* as to how we would communicate with Jarrod. As I worked in the field, I already had some understanding of the cochlear implant, but I needed to find out more. So I set about doing a lot of research and read as much about it as I could.

It was a difficult decision to make, made no easier by the direct statements from medical practitioners who told me that I couldn't have it both ways. It was simply not an option to give him an implant and sign to him, they said! They even told me that if I had him implanted and signed with him, the cochlear centre would withdraw any assistance. Thankfully, I have since heard that mindsets have changed and that the simultaneous use of both communication methods is now more widely accepted.

At that time, research showed that the implant wasn't always successful. So my husband and I decided that the option of signing would be the path that we would take. We knew that Jarrod would learn a natural language without any trouble. This is how we made our choice.

It was important for us that all the people in Jarrod's life learnt to sign and so the lessons began. I taught our friends and family sign language and they can all now sign to some extent. With his limited vocabulary as a toddler, it was relatively easy for people to communicate with him. But as he got older and his language increased, it became trickier for some to keep up with him.

At times there was frustration on both sides, but I'm happy to report that it has become easier to communicate with him because he reads and writes so well. If anyone has an issue with signs, they simply pull out a pen and paper.

My daughter, Alexia, is two and a half years older than Jarrod and before I'd even fallen pregnant with Jarrod, I'd taught her some sign language on account of our deaf friends. So, when Jarrod was diagnosed, it wasn't something completely foreign to her although she did have a few misconceptions. For example, she'd often say things like, 'When I was deaf...' or 'When Jarrod can hear...' It took quite some time – even a few years – for her to work out the status quo.

One time, Jarrod, two, and Alexia, four, were taking a bath together and I poked my head around the door to watch them. Alexia had a toy trumpet in her hand and I noticed her look first at the trumpet then at her brother with earnest. Then, with all her might, she blew the trumpet as loud as she could. Of course Jarrod didn't look up from his activity so she humbly resigned herself to the failure of her experiment by saying, 'Hmmm, well that didn't work.' It made me realise how each of us needed to adjust to our new situation.

Even though I was an interpreter, I felt so naïve and so inexperienced. I'd never worked with any deaf children (only adults), so I had this unquenchable desire to find out all I could about raising them. I devoured books and talked to as many people as I could.

I felt it imperative to see deaf signing children at various ages, so I could get a glimpse of how my child would develop. This, I believe, wasn't only an important step for me, but a necessity for all parents of deaf and hearing impaired children so that they can observe the person their child can become.

At home I read to Jarrod constantly, although not always word for word from the books. I learnt to let him look at the pictures first, allowing him to absorb visual information, then I'd wait for him to look at me to continue. At times, I'd have to prepare the book myself, checking signs and remembering the storyline.

This was very different to my experience with my daughter who loved books from an early age. She and I would read a book for the first time together, whereas for Jarrod, I always had to do my homework first. It took me a while to work through my emotional responses to situations such as these. Sometimes I felt that I was more like his teacher, creating a very structured environment, rather than doing things with him more spontaneously. I fell into the habit of doing recreational activities that would teach him language and benefit him, rather than doing things just for fun.

I stayed away from reading nursery rhymes to Jarrod as you can't sign them with the same patterns. Looking back now, I realise the importance of teaching them to deaf children, even in a different form from what we are used to. Firstly, deaf children can become familiar with common characters which are often referred to throughout life. Secondly, there is a way that you can sign which is poetry and rhythm in itself. But I wasn't aware of this until much later.

I also signed at a normal speed and finger-spelled a lot to him, even as a toddler. I used to ask him if he wanted Vegemite on toast. I'd spell out 'Vegemite' on my hands, knowing that he couldn't reproduce the same word because he was only two years old.

I was very much surprised though, when a couple of months later, I asked him the same question regarding breakfast and he wiggled his fingers in a fashion to resemble the finger-spelling of 'Vegemite'. Wow! I was stoked.

Every time he showed understanding of language, I'd get so excited because it meant that teaching Jarrod sign language was a success. I remember so well the time it dawned on him that the sign, the picture and the written word were all the same object.

We'd been looking at a book, when he turned to me and signed 'kangaroo'. Then he pointed to the picture and signed 'kangaroo'. After that he pointed to the word and signed 'kangaroo'. He beamed and I beamed back and nodded elatedly. He was three years old. We spent the rest of the day going through the same process with different pictures, words and signs.

I think that the use of books, whether reading the words, looking at the pictures or just signing something about what deaf children see is imperative. It gave Jarrod a foundation to learning about the world around him.

I never hid Jarrod's deafness or his sign language from the world. We signed everywhere, in front of anyone. However, this often meant that I had to listen to well-meaning strangers who'd inform me about the cochlear implant, or the need for him to speak, or the potential dangers of signing. Others would say, 'Oh, but he looks so normal!' I knew that most people weren't deliberately being rude, but I became increasingly tired of justifying my parental decisions to the rest of society.

In the end I stopped talking with them. If any comments were made, I simply smiled, thanked them politely and moved on. As much as I wanted to prove to the world that there was nothing deficient about my child, it required far too much energy to keep explaining.

Through my involvement in the field of deafness and hearing impairment, I've seen some deaf adults who have never learnt to deal with the world in which they live and who are reliant on others for almost everything. I've also seen many more who negotiate their way freely and happily around the world. This is what I have always wanted for my son.

So when my cute, blonde-haired four year old said to me that day, 'I can't talk,' I explained in four-year-old terms that communication takes many forms, and although he couldn't produce speech, he could most certainly communicate. Then I showed him how.

We drove down to our local shopping centre where I pretended to be deaf for the whole day. I wrote notes to people, pointed at signs and pictures and gestured my way around the shopping centre in an effort to prove that one doesn't have to speak to get what they want.

While Jarrod was only four, I knew it was critical for him to have a role model from whom he could learn about the world in which he lives. I continued to do 'deaf activities' at different times and still do to this day, although I think I have become more of an embarrassment to him than previously!

As he got older, I began training him to go to the shops and ask for things himself. The first time he did this by himself was a nerve-racking experience for both of us. We were at McDonalds and Jarrod wanted an ice-cream. 'If you want one, Jarrod,' I signed, 'you need to go up and order it yourself.'

He looked at me, shocked and dumbfounded that his mother would even consider being so deliberately cruel to him. I reminded him of the way that he could get an ice-cream – by pointing to his ear and mouthing 'deaf', then by gesturing the concept of ice-cream. He looked terrified and I was worried – but I felt he had to make this crucial step.

I waited at the table, all set to jump up and rescue him if he needed, and watched him take the long walk over to the counter. He kept looking back at me, hoping that I would give him a last minute reprieve, but I kept encouraging him to go.

He walked up to that counter, an eight-year-old boy. He walked away from the counter a 10-foot-tall eight-year-old man, beaming, ice-cream in hand. Since then, he buys his own things, either by pointing at the article, writing it down or gesturing. He is no different to any other boy.

I made it my mission to introduce Jarrod to the Deaf community – children and adults alike. I felt it important that he regularly socialise with other deaf people so that he can feel comfortable and confident with them and with his own identity.

I really believe that deaf people absorb mental energy from being around one another and that continually validates them as people. So we go to as many events as we can find, all organised by the Deaf community, such as theatre, awards nights, story-telling nights and sporting events.

I've noticed that when Jarrod is at a mainstream event with me, he stays close just in case he needs my assistance. As soon as we walk into a deaf event, he is gone without even so much as a glance. It makes me smile, because it means he knows who he is.

At home, I've realised the importance of being seen as Jarrod's mum and not always as his interpreter. So I've encouraged everyone in the family, including my children and stepchildren, to become responsible for their own communication with Jarrod and to learn to sign for themselves. This hasn't been easy to enforce and children being who they are, do not always want to do what they are told, but it has certainly been worth the effort.

Left to right: Jackson, Oren, Jarrod, Tamar, Jaymes and Alexia

'For him, information is knowledge,
is power, is independence.'

Jarrod has become proficient in using the National Relay Service (NRS) to make phone calls so he has a sense of freedom in being able to call others. Technology has been a godsend for many deaf and hearing impaired people and Jarrod is no different. He uses email, MSN, mobile phones and the captions both on TV and at the movies as ways of accessing information. For him, information is knowledge, is power, is independence.

Jarrod is a sporty child and although I'd love for him to be in a deaf team, there aren't enough teams around. Two years ago, he joined the local AFL team and he absolutely loves it. When he first started, I'd interpret the training nights for him because he didn't know the rules of the game. As soon as he felt comfortable, I began to take a back seat.

I wanted him to learn to feel comfortable enough with his teammates to communicate with them through gesturing. This was quite a different situation from going to the shops because communication with teammates is less structured, denser and always contains that possibility of going off on a tangent. Jarrod knew this and so was nervous, but once again made me proud by working through it.

His teammates are great because they immediately accepted his deafness and are willing to gesture to him too. It's hard as a mother to watch your child struggle at times, but the reality is that you, as a mum, aren't always going to be there. Your child has to learn how to work with what they've got. As is said, 'necessity is the mother of invention'. They always work it out!

Although Jarrod doesn't speak and doesn't hear a thing, there are things I've done that I've deemed really important for his development. He goes to speech therapy, not to learn speech as such, but to become phonetically aware of speech patterns which helps him decode unfamiliar words when he reads.

He has acquired a certain understanding of music by taking opportunities to feel instruments as they play, or by feeling the loud speakers which gives him tactile information about music. I talk to him about famous singers and musicians because they come up from time to time in conversation. It's good for deaf kids to know who these people are, not the Elton Johns of my time, but the 50 Cents of today's music scene. Teenagers can't get enough of that sort of stuff!

Jarrod and his best friend Dylan

Just recently, Jarrod said something that made me giggle and smile with pride, knowing that he is comfortable in his own skin. He'd just been stung by a bee and had a mild allergic reaction so that his foot had become swollen.

He looked at me and signed pathetically, 'I'm fed up with having everything wrong with me!'

'What's wrong with you?' I signed.

'I'm allergic to bees and I've got vitiligo,' he signed back despondently.

'No one is perfect,' I said. 'We all have things wrong with us.'

He shook his head vehemently. 'Oh no, my friend Dylan's perfect.'

'There must be something imperfect about Dylan.'

He thought about this long and hard. Then he looked at me earnestly and answered, 'No, he is *perfect!*'

Why is that conversation so moving for me? Firstly, Jarrod never mentioned his friend's deafness as an ailment. And secondly, his 'perfect friend' is also profoundly deaf and uses Auslan as his communication method.

Jarrod does not see his own or other people's deafness as being wrong, deficient or a sign of imperfection.

Now there's a kid who accepts himself for who he is.

5

Deafness is not a disadvantage... just a difference!

Profoundly deaf Olivia Andersen née Gemmell is the founder and CEO of *Hear For You* – a mentoring organisation assisting young deaf people to achieve anything they want in life. After graduating from the University of NSW with a Bachelor degree in Design and a Certificate of Business from RMIT, Olivia's achievements have included working for *marie claire* magazine, backpacking through Europe, Central America and Africa, and winning a Sir Winston Churchill Fellowship. She lives in Sydney with her husband Thomas who is hearing.

PEOPLE OFTEN ASK HOW AND WHAT it is I actually hear. That's not easy to say because I don't know what normal hearing is. I do know, however, that there are many hindrances in being deaf. I find it difficult to follow conversations in a big group. I can't use the telephone normally. It is tough following television and movies without subtitles. I can't hear the words to songs or appreciate music. I would find it difficult to take part in debates or public discussions. Without my hearing aids, I hear no sound at all.

*'I have learned to make my deafness a
learning opportunity rather than a disability.'*

Despite all of that, I have learned to make my deafness a learning opportunity rather than a disability. I have developed ways to compensate by challenging myself to do things in creative and different ways. The skills I have developed as a deaf person have taught me to turn almost any negative into a positive. In many ways, my hearing loss has made me a far stronger person.

When people first learn that I am deaf, many seem to have preconceived ideas as to what my deafness means. I have experienced being dismissed by people who, because of my hearing loss, tend to question my intelligence, abilities and skills.

Despite that, I will never allow others to get me down. Instead, I have always said to myself, 'I am running my own race. I will *not* compete, nor will I compare myself with others.' Accepting who I am has helped me move forward and get on with life.

I was diagnosed as profoundly deaf at eight months old. My parents had an ABO blood incompatibility and I became jaundiced after I was born, which required a blood exchange when I was three days old. It was always assumed that the jaundice caused my deafness, although recent tests, despite being inconclusive, suggest that it could be genetic.

Specialist doctors told my parents that I'd never be able to speak nor go to a mainstream school. Thankfully Mum and Dad had the attitude that anything could be achieved with the right support and speech therapy. So immediately they enrolled me at The Shepherd Centre in its early intervention program for deaf children. I also had weekly speech lessons at an Australian hearing centre with Margaret Colebrook with whom I'm still in close contact. Margaret is the founder of *Let Us Hear*, an organisation which endeavours to get financial support from the government for deaf people over the age of 21.

Growing up, my mother and I were always incredibly close. She put in a massive amount of hard work and always told me,

Mum and me

'Olivia, life is what you make it.' It was often hard for her. She used to worry that over the years she had become more like a teacher than a mother to me. But her love and encouragement helped me no end, especially when it came to my hearing loss.

Dad was always a great support, particularly in my sporting activities. He coached me in cricket, tennis and athletics, which helped my confidence enormously. When I was a baby he would sing to me through my hearing aids as he walked along, holding me in his arms.

At 11 years old, I felt burnt out, exhausted from the constant speech therapy, the extra school work and the intense concentration. One evening, I withdrew from the family dinner table, went upstairs to my room and wrote a letter to 'Goddy' in order to pour out my feelings. I wrote:

Dear Goddy

I don't want to hurt your feelings. But I don't want to be deaf. It is too hard for me. Goddy please let me hear without any hearing aids before I die because I want to have a try. Could you do that? Hope you can. I feel so tired. How is life there? Hope it is okay. How are the angels? Love Olivia.

Mum gave this letter to my teacher at the time, who had

Me at 11 years old with our family dog, Murphy

it published in *The Sydney Morning Herald*. A few days later, a delightfully decorated parchment scroll arrived in our letterbox with a reply handwritten in gold.

Dear Olivia, Life here in heaven is very good and all the angels are well. One special angel, Acoustica, has read your letter and she wants you to know that she can't hear very well either but Goddy has given her long legs to run like the wind and beautiful strong arms to swim like a fish and golden wings to soar like an eagle. What she enjoys most is turning off her hearing aid when all the other angels are bickering and enjoying all the peace, love and hope that only Goddy can put into one's heart. Goddy knows you will always hear Him in your heart even when you are tired. And who knows, one day just maybe, you and the good angel, Acoustica, can throw away those hearing aids forever. All my love, Goddy.

This letter was also printed in *The Sydney Morning Herald* and the correspondence received an overwhelming response from readers, some of whom wanted to know if I was able to hear yet! My words had been a plea from the heart as I struggled to understand why I was the only one in my school who was deaf. But to receive the letter and read about 'Angel Acoustica' helped me feel that I was not alone in those feelings. Over the years, I have learnt that we are humans first and foremost. Whatever differences we have come second. Eighteen years later, I completely accept and embrace my hearing loss.

Clockwise from left: Mum, Dad, Sophie, Angus, Forbes and me, 1990

I have been blessed with a close, loving family and I suppose I am fortunate in being the youngest of four. I have always looked up to my older siblings as role models. Angus, Sophie and Forbes all have integrity, a good sense of humour, live life to the full and are affectionate and kind. While both boys are very adventurous and have pushed the boundaries in their travels, which I have always admired, Sophie has a huge heart and used to work as a fundraiser with a charity assisting disadvantaged youth, which I have always found inspirational. All have given me support and encouragement along the way.

I attended first the local pre-school and later a deaf unit at a local primary school. My parents became concerned about the then lack of integration with the hearing students. So they moved me to a small private prep school, where I received support from The Shepherd Centre.

I spent my prep and junior school years at a private school for girls where I once again received first-rate support from The Shepherd Centre as well as the staff who taught me. But their senior school was highly competitive and with 240 girls in

each year, my parents felt it would not be suitable for me.
After a number of letters (and Mum's tears on the phone when
she was told that their books were full), they moved me to a
Catholic girls' school, Loreto Kirribilli, where I had the support
of an itinerant teacher from the Royal Institute for Deaf and
Blind Children.

I was incredibly happy in the special, caring, community-
minded atmosphere of Loreto. Being a real lover of sports, I was
fortunate to have a sporty group in my year and playing lots of
team sports helped me make friends. I ended up representing
the school in a variety of team and individual sports and had
some great successes, particularly in winning the state Catholic
schools' netball and cricket
competitions.

Throughout my school life,
I persisted with speech and
drama lessons, which helped
improve the tone and animation
in my voice. One of Mum and
Dad's proudest memories was
the day I was awarded a credit
at the Sydney Eisteddfod for
*My Year 12 Geography class
(me, in front, second from right)*

reciting a poem. The examiner had not even been aware that
I was deaf! Such a feat could largely be attributed, I feel, not
only to the countless hours spent rehearsing the poem, but
also to the thousands of hours devoted to practising my verbal
communication combined with the speech therapy I'd had as
a child.

I also made an effort to write using correct grammar so that
I could learn to enjoy expressing myself through the written
word. I tried to talk to as many people as possible, to read
newspapers and to watch the daily news, which fortunately by

Winning the netball finals, 1998
(me, second from right)

then had subtitles. I knew that the more information I could acquire, the more confidence I would gain in forming and expressing my own opinions which could only improve my school work and many other areas of my life.

I participated in extra-curricular school activities, including completing the Gold Duke of Edinburgh Award which involved a combination of physical fitness, community service and developing life skills. There was also a residential project and two four-day adventure camps. I found the program challenging and beneficial in so many ways. It helped me gain confidence, use my initiative, face hurdles and accept responsibility for things in my life.

I recall one night during the hiking camp when we were all sitting around the campfire after a particularly strenuous day. I had just prepared my hearing aids and without thinking threw my old batteries into the flames. Everyone around me suddenly leapt up. 'What's going on, guys?' I asked innocently, to which I lipread them shout, 'Explosion!' They'd thought that someone had been shooting at us in the bush. I hadn't heard a thing!

During my last year of school, I suffered frequent attacks of Menieres which were at their worst before exams and assessments. For a while, I thought that I'd be unable to sit the HSC exams. Fortunately the attacks responded to treatment and I completed my HSC, obtaining marks good enough to go to university. I was also presented, during my final school year, with the School President's Award for Spirit and Service

– in recognition of Outstanding Contribution and Participation in School Activities. These were some of my life's most memorable moments.

A month after leaving school, I worked behind the bar of a busy hotel. In the noisy environment, communication challenges were far worse than they'd been in the classroom. But I was never one to buckle under the pressure of an obstacle. I recall the night I was confronted by a group of drunken men who, unaware that I was deaf, were relentless in their demands for rounds of beer. Hearing them was impossible because of the deafening background noise. There was no way of lipreading them due to the distorted way in which they slurred their speech. Ironically, it was actually their inebriation that saved me, because they staggered away happily with drinks they hadn't even ordered!

In 1999, I joined Palm Beach Surf Lifesaving Club and became the second deaf lifesaver in Australia at that time. I undertook patrols, helped out at social functions, competed in swims and surfing events and did my First Aid, Bronze Medallion and Advanced Resuscitation

Surf lifesaving at Palm Beach

Certificates. This involved a huge commitment, which included my often having to stay over at the clubhouse. They were incredible seasons, which cultivated my courage and enthusiasm and further expanded my circle of friends.

I recall the day when my heightened intuition and acute ability to read body language (one of the benefits of my hearing loss) saved my life. I was on patrol, swimming out in the surf, way beyond the breakers, enjoying my own silence, when I became aware of a sensation that something wasn't quite right. I turned to see a mass of backs – my fellow swimmers – heading back to shore. It didn't take long to realise a shark alarm had been raised and I'd been the only one not to have heard it. Without those 'gifts', I doubt I would even reacted at all and who knows what would have been my fate!

In 1999 I began studying Business at the Australian Catholic University, but suffered terribly from a lack of specialist support. When my mother rang to express concern about the fact that I did not even have a notetaker, she was told rather dismissively, 'We prefer our students to be autonomous.' I think that perhaps a mentor's intervention might have been more seriously regarded than what must have appeared to them to be an overly anxious mother.

With my parents at my graduation

Without support, it became increasingly difficult and halfway through the year, I transferred to the University of New South Wales to study my Bachelor of Design. Again, I was faced with the same predicament. But this time, I wasn't going to let them win that easily. Four years of perseverance later I went on to get my degree. In hindsight, now that I know that universities receive special government grants to support disabled students, I should have been stronger in pressing for a notetaker. In fact, I should have threatened to take the issue to the Equal Opportunities Tribunal. If only I'd known then what I know now...

During this time, I did some work experience associated with my Design degree, including designing layouts and setting up fashion editorial shoots for fashion magazines *Vogue* and *ELLE*. I was also fortunate to get a position with the fashion magazine, *marie claire*, where I designed layouts for their Lifestyle, Travel and Fashion Insiders, set up their monthly layout board, and participated in the decision making of the magazine's structure. This set me up really well in terms of my career.

While I met some amazing people there, the only downside was a superior who was often inconsiderate and impatient towards me. On one occasion when I was speaking to her about work, she quickly looked away to a colleague and asked, 'What did she say?' I confronted her and explained how her dismissiveness made me feel. From then on she was more considerate, I think because I'd earned her respect from being so open with her about my feelings.

My advice to deaf children and teenagers is learn to be bold in your actions and ask for cooperation. You may be surprised at how others respond. Having a sense of humour definitely helps. If you can lighten up, laugh at

My marie claire *portfolio*

*'...learn to be bold in your actions
and ask for cooperation.'*

yourself and your mistakes, and see the funny side of your deafness without belittling yourself, you will become someone others enjoy being around.

I have always felt it important to take myself out of my square. At 23, I left home to explore the world, live independently and let my spirit roam free. But I received a nasty shock when I first moved to London and began applying for jobs. As soon as I mentioned that I was deaf, my applications resulted in no further response. What was I to do? I couldn't use the phone to make appointments.

It didn't take me long to grasp that if I wanted a job, I was going to have to challenge people's preconceptions as to what deafness was. So I began the process of travelling to job agencies on the London underground, presenting myself in person so that people could judge me face to face.

My luck changed and I got a great job offer. Endeavouring to be pleasant and personable certainly helped too. I do not expect hearing people to accommodate my needs but I feel it is my responsibility to show them that I am capable of doing anything requested of me and to dispel any other concerns they have about my hearing loss.

During my three-year stint in London, I worked as a features contributor, photographer and designer for the lifestyle and fitness magazine, *Shape Up*. My role involved coming up with a story idea, putting in a proposal to the editor, then carrying out all the artwork and photo shoots in order to bring it to press.

Some of my assignments took me to New York, Norway and all over England. It was one of the most exhilarating periods of my career.

Growing up, I always felt that I was different. I did not belong to the Deaf community because I did not know sign language. I was a deaf person living in the hearing world relying on spoken language and hearing aids. I always felt in between two worlds because I was neither 'hearing' nor 'signing'.

Because of this I wanted to further explore and develop my own identity. One way of doing this, I thought, was to travel alone with international strangers who spoke English as their second language, and would therefore feel a little different themselves in

foreign environments. So after travelling through Europe and Central America with friends from London, I decided to backpack through Africa.

In Nairobi I joined a group of international backpackers and embarked on a six-week truck camping trip through Kenya, Tanzania, Zanzibar, Malawi, Zambia and Zimbabwe. It was one of the most challenging periods of my life. At times, I found it arduous trying to get my message across, but I was always quietly assertive in asking the others for their consideration in things.

On my travels in Africa – Kenya, October 2004

For example, when we sat around the campfire chatting, I asked the group to pass a torch around to each person who spoke to enable me to lipread. The trip helped develop my strength of character and to be my own person. I must confess to switching my hearing aids off the night I heard a group of hyenas howling outside the tent!

In my mind, assertiveness is being neither aggressive nor submissive. I may not always get what I want but I always feel a sense of satisfaction in letting the other person know how I am feeling.

In work and social situations I always try, whenever necessary, to choose a seating position with less background noise and the best possible lighting. As a deaf person, I am very aware of body language and am able to 'read' people which enables me to decide whether or not it is worthwhile giving energy to the person. With this skill, I have learnt how to choose friends who have empathy and who respect me as a person. I have found that deaf people tend to make friends with genuine, special and worthwhile people. Somehow a deaf person often attracts the right people. As friendships are so important, this can go a long way towards living a happy life.

This was certainly the case with meeting Thomas, a very special man, who is now my husband. He has since told me that he was initially interested in me because of my strength of character and the dignified way in which I handled my deafness.

The first night we met, he thought I had an accent, but could not identify which country it came from! I told him I was Australian, but he looked at me doubtfully. 'I lipread,' I said, and then the penny dropped! After more polite conversation and a few nervous laughs, we took to the dance floor. Because the music was slow, I had trouble following the beat and felt awkward. Thomas noticed and pulled me closer, placing his hand on my shoulder where his fingers began to tap out the rhythm; a considerate gesture that, lucky for me, was to be the first of many.

Seven years later in June 2007, Thomas chose a picturesque valley in the Tuscan Hills of Italy overlooking a medieval village, to propose to me. A year later we were married in my old school chapel at Loreto Kirribilli, followed by an unforgettable reception with our family and friends at the Blue Room, a glass vessel which circles the Sydney Harbour.

Thomas is Danish, so with family and friends coming from Denmark to our wedding, I decided to surprise them (and my new husband!) with a five minute bridal speech in Danish. Danish is often likened to 'speaking with a potato in the throat', so much lipreading and listening to my Danish friend was involved in order to perfect the pronunciation. I believe my years of speech therapy contributed a lot to my being able to achieve this. It is important to me that our children speak Danish and it is my goal to learn this with them.

I feel fortunate to have found someone like Thomas. I love him for the person he is, for his personality, charm, intellect and patience and the consideration he gives towards my hearing loss. When I am unable to communicate by email or SMS, Thomas will

Thomas and me on our wedding day

make a phone call on my behalf. He will also relay telephone conversations so I can communicate with the person on the other end. When he wants to get my attention, he has a form of a 'cooee' call that is pitched at the right level for me to hear and respond. Whilst I am very fortunate to have his support, I still highly value my independence. I feel empowered when I challenge and assert myself. I also enjoy all the things we do and decisions we make jointly. I try not to burden him with any hearing loss problems.

Perhaps you think that I have been one of the 'lucky' deaf people who have escaped the difficult challenges of being deaf, but believe me, I have had my fair share of negative experiences. It still hurts when I remember a number of incidents that happened during my senior school years.

As a girl, I experienced meanness and bitchiness more than physical bullying. I once overheard a school playground discussion about who would be the next sports captain. Three of my friends thought I would be selected, but another girl who desperately wanted the captaincy said that this would be unlikely because I wouldn't be able to make speeches. She then imitated my voice in an exaggerated, ugly way. Unfortunately I heard. I was shattered.

Another time I was on a ski chairlift with a friend when all of a sudden I heard this dreadful noise. I was anxious that something had gone wrong with the chairlift. When I asked my friend, she said she didn't know what I was talking about. The noise kept going and I was confused. Eventually, I noticed that my friend was smirking with her lips pressed together and I realised that she had been making the noise. To her, it was amusing, but I found it distressing, callous and unkind.

The benefit of life experience is a wonderful thing. I realise now that I should never have let these things upset me. I

'I realise now that the only way to deal with bullies is by questioning, reasoning, standing firm and confronting without being aggressive.'

should have either challenged the perpetrators or rationalised that they were the ones with the problem and not have taken it so personally. Bullying and bitchiness are merely signs of cowardice and immaturity. I realise now that the only way to deal with bullies is by questioning, reasoning, standing firm and confronting without being aggressive. Difficult to do, I know, when you're a teenager. But it's worth giving it a go.

Adolescence is such an unsettled time with hormonal change and development. It is often extremely difficult for deaf teenagers who may have not developed the life skills to cope with these turbulent changes in their lives. It is for this reason that in 2007 I began setting up a first-of-its-kind mentoring organisation in Australia called *Hear For You* for young deaf people attending mainstream schools.

My research revealed that when a child is diagnosed as deaf, the primary concerns of most parents are: will my child hold their own in mainstream society? Will my child have a normal career? Will my child be happy in life and have normal relationships? Experiences internationally show that involvement with a deaf adult mentor can alleviate these concerns and enable parents to work more effectively with their child, which has long-term benefits for the child.

A deaf mentor, who has experienced life's ups and downs, can instil in a young deaf person the desire to believe – 'If he or she can, so can I!' A hearing person, even with the best of intentions, cannot provide such an example.

Hear For You, a non-profit organisation, provides e-mentoring (online communication) and workshops aimed at helping young deaf people to engage fully in life and realise their potential. Some of the workshops' topics include identity, social and conversational skills, assertiveness, leadership, positive thinking and future prospects. The workshops deal with ways to break down the barriers of people's preconceptions about deafness, how to handle group discussions and to learn confidence in expressing opinions. Feelings of not belonging in the community and lack of self-worth are discussed, along with tactics to overcome these. We also do role-playing scenarios to help deal with difficult situations. The workshops encourage better vocational aspirations and have a positive effect on the adolescents' motivation and confidence and thus help equip them with the skills to lead happy and fulfilled social and working lives.

My own experiences in adolescence were not my only motivation to set up *Hear For You*. One of my greatest sources of inspiration came nearly ten years ago from an encounter I had with a mother of a deaf baby in a waiting room at a hearing centre in Sydney. The mother had just learned that her baby's hearing was impaired. Just as I was walking out of a hearing test appointment, she must have noticed my hearing aids because she approached me with tears in her eyes.

'Please help me!' she begged. 'My baby is deaf. I need to know! Will she lead a normal life?' It was clear that she'd never spoken to anyone with a hearing loss before and desperately needed reassurance that things would be okay. All I could say was, 'Trust me. It will be okay. You will pull through just like my mother and I did,' and I smiled. It seemed to have a profound effect. Her face immediately relaxed. The incident always remained deeply ingrained in me. I would have liked to have helped her more.

Much of my inspiration I also attribute to my great grandmother, Jessie Street, who was a joint initiator of the 1967 Referendum which amended the Australian Constitution to give Aborigines the right to vote. Her life was dedicated to peace and justice and she did much work for the under-privileged and disadvantaged.

It was while reading her autobiography overseas that I became aware that I simply had to devote my life to helping enhance the lives of young deaf people and their families. The realisation was so profound that I decided to quit my job in the magazine industry in London and return to Australia to put my life purpose into practice.

In July 2007, I was awarded a Winston Churchill Memorial Trust Fellowship at Government House. The Fellowship provides the opportunity and financial means to undertake an area of study overseas that is not available in Australia. The aim of my Fellowship was to study overseas mentoring programs and workshop activities in the area of confidence building, empowerment and leadership for young deaf people here in Australia.

During one of the interviews in a fairly gruelling selection process that lasted six months (culminating in a final interview before a selection panel of 22 people), the chairman asked me a question from the far end of the table where it was hard to read his lips. I thought then that it was all over when I was forced to say, 'I'm sorry. I can't hear you nor can I read your lips. Please repeat the question' and he was obliged to ask someone next to me to repeat it. But this was not the case! Not only did I succeed in being one of the 25 people selected from the 500 applicants in the state, but I was the only one to receive The Sir William Kilpatrick Churchill Fellowship, given once a year in honour of someone who is considered to be 'the father of the Churchill Trust in Australia'.

My motto is 'with the right mindset, anything is possible'.

My five weeks overseas took me to the US, UK and Scandinavia where I learned many new skills to help teens deal with all manner of life situations. I was then able to share these with fellow mentors at *Hear For You* and integrate them into our organisation's program structure and content. So far, our pilot workshops have been very successful – the participants were motivated and excited. In fact, one of the teenagers even went back to school and approached his sports master about becoming a team captain! It confirmed our view that there is a real need for something like this for young deaf people.

People are often intrigued by the way I communicate and how I cope with life, but more than ever these days, I feel that my difference is accepted by others. Perhaps it is because I view deafness as a challenge and have developed skills to overcome the obvious barriers that are naturally associated with it. What I do know is that I continuously remind myself that there is no point dwelling on the negatives and that I have so many positive things in my life to be grateful for. My motto is 'with the right mindset, anything is possible'. To me, deafness is not a disadvantage ... just a difference!

6

Why strive to survive when you can do so much better?

Roz Keenan is mother to nine-year-old Sarah, profoundly deaf. Sarah wears a hearing aid and has a cochlear implant. She uses speech and sign to communicate and attends a mainstream school with her hearing brother and sister. Roz works as national parent coordinator at Deaf Children Australia and loves advocating for the needs of deaf and hard of hearing children. The family live in Diamond Creek, Melbourne with Sarah's dad John, sister Emma and brother Jack.

'WELL, YOU CAN SEE on the screen, your daughter has absolutely no hearing. She's profoundly deaf.'

These are words I will never forget. They sent my whole body spinning and all I could do was cry. From that moment on my world changed direction.

After eight months of testing, four audiograms and Auditory Brainstem Response testing, we finally had a diagnosis. Up until then, our little girl had baffled paediatric audiologists, none of whom could confirm whether she was deaf or simply being temperamental. Now, we knew that our beautiful baby girl hadn't heard a thing we'd been saying to her or what had been happening around her for the first 16 months of her life.

My mind raced into the future. Would she have friends?, Would she drive a car?, Would she get married? Would she have children?

At the time, my husband John was away in Stradbroke Island on business. When he rang to ask about the results, I couldn't even speak. 'Are you still there?' he asked. When I mumbled yes, he said, 'I'm coming home. I'll see you in the morning.'

Neither of us had wanted to admit that there'd been anything wrong, but deep down I'm sure we both knew.

In hindsight, there were clues. She'd go to sleep if we settled her by touch. She'd crawl crying down the hallway of our old house and verbal attempts to comfort her would be in vain. Until I'd lean down and touch her which would scare the wits out of her.

Driving home from the hospital, my mum and I hardly spoke. When I picked Emma up from my mum's, my stepfather asked us what had happened. That's when it really started to sink in. My stepfather said, 'Methodist Ladies College has a really good deaf program. Maybe she can go to school there.' His hearing daughters had gone there. That only made me cry harder.

When John arrived home, we hardly spoke a word. We simply moved around each other in silence, too afraid of what might happen if we opened our mouths. Neither of us knew how to articulate what we were feeling or what the next steps would be.

After the initial shock of the diagnosis, we were soon caught up in the barrage of appointments which threatened to swallow us up. Within a week, Sarah had her first hearing aid moulds cast and we'd seen one of Melbourne top ENT surgeons to check the anatomy of her ears and talk about 'possibilities' for Sarah.

By the following week, she'd had her first hearing aids fitted. That was the biggest shock ... my little baby girl wearing hearing aids. It was all happening so fast. In just two weeks, we'd gone from being in the dark to Sarah getting hearing aids and were now travelling rapidly down the road to ... *where?*

What struck me was the lack of information given to you. They said, 'Oh, you're here to have your daughter's hearing aid moulds cast!', assuming that we were fully informed about the choices and the different avenues to take. They gave us the 'pink book', as I call it, of information about early intervention services, that was supposed to tell you everything about hearing loss. It didn't. And that was it. It was all so clinical. That is why my greatest passion has become ensuring parents receive all the information about the different options so that they can make fully informed decisions.

Sitting in the car on the way home, I stared down at the 'pink book' in my lap. 'I guess we should read it and find out what we need to do,' I whispered to John. It was a defining moment – an acknowledgement that we knew we needed to take matters into our own hands.

The experience evoked memories of a hearing girl I'd known growing up. Her whole family was deaf and used Auslan. Both parents worked and drove cars, while her brother studied at university and worked part-time at a furniture factory.

It was comforting to know that deaf people could be active participants in the community just like everybody else and that their deafness made little difference to their quality of life. I began to realise that Sarah would be okay. Her journey would simply be different from what I had imagined for her.

I will never forget the day Sarah received her hearing aids. The second she put them on, her face sparked up. After 15 months of vacant looks, at last she was taking things in. After that, there was never any trouble with her refusing to wear her aids. She was in no doubt that they were her only access to the hearing world.

By connecting Sarah's hearing aid to a long tube-like object called a 'stethoclip', I was able to hear what Sarah could hear through her aid. Standing in the kitchen, I heard the loudest hum and buzz and thought, 'What on earth is that?', only to realise it was our microwave!

My thought was, 'You poor kid! Fancy trying to distinguish between me talking to you and the microwave or the fan, or the TV or the radio or the conversations happening in the background.'

Rather synchronistically, a couple of weeks later, I ran into a friend who had just retired as a special education teacher. She'd heard about Sarah and asked me how I was. I replied, 'It's all so new. I don't know what I'm doing or where I'm going.' She told me that if I wished, I was welcome to come and get any of her resources from working for 30 years in the field.

On saying goodbye, she smiled and said, 'Good luck with the political battle.' I was puzzled. But after a few phone calls to the early intervention services, it began to make sense. Each service had its own approach, which made decisions as to where you wanted to go all the more bewildering.

Early intervention

Of all the questions you ask yourself about deafness, the question 'Where would she go to school?' worried me the most. As an early childhood educator, I'd worked in 'special schools', but Sarah certainly didn't fit that criteria. I knew Sarah wouldn't achieve her potential, unless she received the right assistance.

At that time, there were three early intervention choices. One was the state-wide, government-funded, free early intervention program for children with hearing loss. The second was a privately-funded early intervention service. The third was the Department of Human Services home-based early intervention service. There was a fourth option – the Early Education Program – but it was on the opposite side of town to us.

We eventually decided on the government-funded one that offered the bilingual approach. This meant that we would teach Sarah to sign and, if possible, talk so she could make an informed choice once she was older about what mode she preferred. The approach seemed to open a lot more doors without us having to narrow ourselves down to one option when we knew nothing about any of them. All of a sudden, I felt a whole lot better.

Sarah began at the Monnington playgroup, where kids were encouraged to communicate in either English or Auslan through age-appropriate activities. Parents were persuaded to stay and share with other parents what was going on at home. I found it hugely positive getting to know people who were trying to deal with the same experiences as I was, while having professionals on hand you could turn to for expert advice.

What daunted me most was establishing what was appropriate for a child who was behind her hearing peers in terms of language development. With a hearing child, I knew which milestones to aim for. With a deaf child it was a whole different ball game.

Sarah had been deprived of the 16 months of incidental learning that a hearing child has from birth. My job as a parent became to 'teach' her about the sounds around her and help her learn the world and its language to which she hadn't had access.

Besides the playgroup, a teacher of the deaf (TOD) and/ or a psychologist from Monnington visited us at home on a fortnightly basis. Rather than working directly with Sarah, we decided that the best use of the hour would be discussing the best ways we (her family) could support her.

The emphasis was always on teaching us how to teach her. One week, we'd ask the TOD, 'How are we going to teach Sarah colours?', and she'd run us through the process, while Sarah drew colours beside us, actively involved. At the next visit, the TOD worked with Sarah while the psychologist helped me create a six month educational plan for her then discussed how we were going to achieve each goal.

They taught us all about visual communication. We learnt to get Sarah's attention by tapping her on the shoulder to ensure that she was looking at us, to move objects off the dining table so she was able to see the person at the other end and to slow down our speech and speak clearly when talking to her.

Rather than mumbling when we were in a hurry, we were trained to stop and think about what we wanted to say before relaying it to Sarah. If she looked as though she didn't understand, we learned to repeat things in different ways until she did.

It was a methodical process. I re-discovered the importance of reading and storytelling in order to promote language learning in both English and Auslan. Thereafter, if I was ever going somewhere, I'd take my camera and would photograph what I saw. These photos formed the basis for many picture books which I'd then create for Sarah and later discuss at the dining room table while she'd learn all the associated words.

Even now, I still use pre-learning with Sarah. The teachers always send me the curriculum that Sarah will be learning that semester. Then immediately we set about using all the language, in both Auslan and English, so that she becomes able to access all activities that most of the other kids so easily grasp.

During our intervention program, we received access to a social worker, a community worker and a speech therapist.

This could have extended to an occupational or physiotherapist depending on needs, but Sarah didn't require one. Our community worker was deaf, so we learnt to bounce off her about all things deaf and about her strategies growing up.

When Sarah was three, we began attending a new group called The Language Enrichment Group. Still part of Monnington, this was specifically designed for three-year-old hearing and deaf children to work together side by side in a language-rich visual and aural environment.

It consisted of an equal balance of English speaking kids and Auslan-using kids who were taught by both an English speaking teacher and an Auslan teacher. In this way both languages were used simultaneously.

Aside from that, Sarah attended her local kinder so that she could enjoy a combination of deaf friends from early intervention and hearing peers from her local area. It has always been important to us that she have both hearing and deaf friends. To this day, we make sure that she still gets to see her deaf friends from her early intervention. They have such a special bond.

When she turned four, she did two sessions at regular kinder with no assistance and one full day at a Junior School for the Deaf where she got her bilingual access.

I didn't put her in for longer than a day because that was exhausting enough for such a little girl and the brain overload was huge. Often she'd come home asleep in the back of the taxi and the driver would have to carry her to our front door.

The support we received during our years at Monnington was amazing. While the emphasis was always on the outcomes for Sarah, the greatest learning was most definitely had by both John and me.

As newbies to this world, we discovered just how many questions had to be answered when it came to options for deaf and hard of hearing children. Should they learn to sign? Would technology assist them? Will they have spoken language? Is deafness or hearing loss the only factor here?

We, like most hearing parents of children with hearing loss, are haunted by the number of decisions we are required

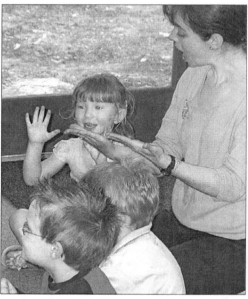

Sarah at The Language Enrichment Group, Monnington

to make, with such little knowledge. One of the psychologists at Monnington summed it up for me one day when she said, 'When your children turn 21 and they look back at photos, they will laugh and say, "Why did you dress me in that?" It was because at the time that seemed like the right decision. Make your decisions now on what feels right and never be afraid to reassess and change as the situation changes. What works for you now might not work for anyone else, or for you in six months time.'

Learning Auslan

To help Sarah's bilingual communication, I wanted our whole family to learn to sign. Within two weeks of the diagnosis, my stepsister – a speech therapist – gave me an old Signed English dictionary and I dragged out my old Auslan alphabet chart I'd had from school days so we could practise with those.

Later, I met a lady who was deaf at our local Living and Learning Centre who spoke and signed. For several weeks, she came to our home to teach my extended family and some of Sarah's childcare workers to sign.

I'm not as fluent in Auslan as I need to be because Sarah won't sign with me. She always says, 'Mum, you can hear me talk. You don't need me to sign!' Yet, if we go anywhere where there are deaf adults, she'll always sign with *them*.

At the recent VicDeaf Christmas rally, a man began signing and talking to her. She turned to me and asked, 'Mum, is he hearing or deaf?'

'Deaf,' I replied. Within an instant, she had turned off her voice and had begun signing.

Nonetheless, she is quick to give me feedback on my signing skills and is always correcting my Auslan. 'That's not right, Mum!' she'll say. 'That sign's an old one!' or 'That's a signed English one!' Sarah so capably swaps between the two worlds now, a skill I am envious of.

Getting the cochlear implant

At the age of four Sarah's hearing dropped out of the speech range in her left ear, even with assistance from the most powerful hearing aids. We decided to investigate the possibility of her having a cochlear implant. The ear, nose and throat specialist informed us that Sarah would be a good candidate for an implant due to her profound hearing loss of 90–120 decibels and the fact that she was showing signs of speech with a hearing aid.

One night the medical show *RPA* showed a cochlear implant operation on an adult, so I forced myself to watch it. I'm not great with blood at the best of times, but I found it gruesome. What horrified me most was the drilling into the skull and having to put my baby to sleep. Could we really put our little girl through this? What benefit would it be to her?

The cochlear implant would get Sarah into the speech range, we were told. Yet audiograms revealed that she was already achieving this with her hearing aid on the right side. Hearing aids would only improve with the advancement of technology. It was a decision I anguished over.

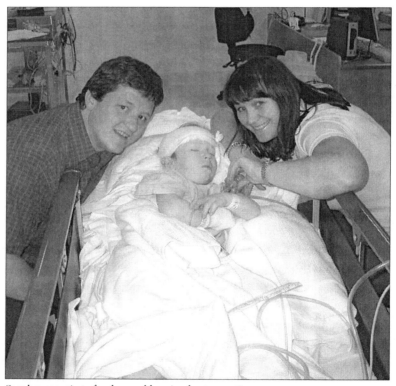

Sarah recovering after her cochlear implant operation

Once it was determined that she had no more hearing to lose and that outer technology (a hearing aid) wasn't going to help, the cochlear option began to look more and more attractive.

Sarah was four and a half when she was fitted with an implant. As soon as we told people, they said, 'Oh, how wonderful it will be to watch it be switched on!' But what an anti-climax it was! Sarah's face didn't light up and she didn't say, 'Hi Mum. It's great to finally hear you!'

There is a big difference between turning on an implant with someone who has never had clarity of sound and someone who previously had their hearing, then lost it. This was demonstrated on the TV program *Australian Story* where they featured a lady who received an implant after losing her hearing. On the way home, she heard a clicking sound in the car then realised it was the indicator.

But for Sarah, who'd never experienced clarity of sound, trying to distinguish what sound went with what person, object, or action in those first few days and weeks must have been frightening and exhausting.

She'd put a texta onto paper, listen to it, stop, look at the texta, look at the paper then eventually realise the texta was making the sound when she scribbled it across the paper. Then there were the leaves in the trees and the plastic shopping bags that rustled, those incidental sounds that we take for granted that hearing people would naturally tune out to, that Sarah would point out to me.

With all this going on for Sarah, I began to wonder what she actually heard through her implant. As a hearing person, I was able to hear that the hearing aid was amplifying the sound for her. The speech processor, on the other hand, takes in sound and breaks it into electrical impulses, transmitting it to the cochlear implant. Without my having both the internal and external parts, it would be impossible for me to hear as Sarah would.

An expert once related what Sarah might hear in this way: 'You know when a person has injured their voice box and talks with a handheld amplifier placed at their throat which produces a very clinical, computerised sound? Well, that's what Sarah hears through the implant.' I realised that my daughter had never heard my natural voice – only a computerised version.

Roz with Sarah (four and a half)

Being your child's advocate

In raising a deaf child, I've encountered many barriers, many of which will happily remain if you choose to leave them there. In challenging them, they often disappear.

When I get a 'no', I instantly reel back, but then think, 'How can I get around this?' If you do some research, you'll always find a loophole or another way of getting to 'yes'.

I always tell parents, 'You're the only constant advocate in your child's life, the only single case manager they'll have through their lives.' As much as I rely on professionals, they come and go. When Sarah leaves the school grounds, it's no longer their problem. As a parent, you're the one who wants to see your child grow and develop and hit all of the targets.

One of the keys to being successful in raising a deaf child is developing the confidence to ask for things. If you don't ask, your child won't get. Simple as that! If you're not happy with something, don't moan about it to others. Go and tell the person directly and ask for what you want. You will very often get it!

You have to build your own confidence to know that it's your right to look after your children and it's your child's right to have you ask all the hard questions. Teachers aren't going to ask them. If you don't have the confidence to ask the hard questions, find someone who is. Make it someone objective; take a neutral friend who won't let it impact them if they don't get what you asked for.

This was no more clearly demonstrated than when choosing a school for Sarah. We made the decision to enrol her at her local primary school, Diamond Creek East Primary, mainly so she'd be with her big sister and the same kids she'd been with from the age of three. These kids had watched her grow, from seeing her wearing bilateral hearing aids to getting the implant in kinder, from babbling in unintelligible speech to reading out loud in class. They accepted her warts and all, so to speak.

'One of the keys to being successful in raising a deaf child is developing the confidence to ask for things. If you don't ask, your child won't get. Simple as that!'

When Sarah had been a baby, I'd always expected she would go to a deaf facility because then she'd be with other deaf children and have the specialist support from a teacher of the deaf. I had steered away from the local school through a conviction that a visiting teacher who came to the school just a few hours a week would never be enough support to integrate her into the local primary school.

Over the years, my opinion changed. In some cases, deaf kids, I realised, were removed from the classroom to be taught by their teacher of the deaf. Whereas, at her local school, she'd remain in the classroom while her visiting teacher assisted her with what the rest of the class were doing.

However, to make absolutely sure that Sarah would get the best support, I left no stone unturned. I worked with the school principal on what we could do to meet Sarah's needs for a whole *two years* prior to her starting at the school.

In Victoria, there is an education needs questionnaire you fill out before you start at a school which forms the basis for which level of funding your child will receive there.

There are six levels of funding which range from Level One (the lowest level) to Level Six (the highest). Level Six is generally for kids who need someone to care for them 24/7 and are a risk to themselves and others.

When the funding comes in from the government, it is the school's responsibility to notify you of what level your child will receive. Hardly ever are you informed of the exact figure or what this will equate to in terms of support for your child other than in hours of support.

But you as a parent have every right to ask how much funding the government has allocated as well as challenge both the school and the government on how much support they are willing to provide. We were informed that Sarah was going to receive Level Two funding on the last day of term, right before Christmas break, just a month before she was to start Prep. Level Two funding meant that Sarah would be given an integration aide for approximately 10 hours a week. The aide she had been allocated had no Auslan skills. I was furious. So the school lodged our appeal, a process which would hang over us through the Christmas break.

There was no doubt about it. I wanted an aide with Auslan – nothing else would do for her – for more than 10 hours a week.

The assistant principal informed me, however, that I shouldn't worry, because Sarah's aide would get six months of professional development and she'd be up to speed with Sarah.

This made me even more incensed. Auslan was Sarah's first language! She would run rings around an aide with no Auslan even with six months under their belt.

'That is unacceptable,' I complained. 'She's not being given a fair go in the classroom among the other kids. Does that mean that in six months, I can go to the Department and tell them that my child has been disadvantaged for the past six months because she hasn't been able to access her school work and request a new aide?'

'Yes,' the assistant principal said.

I knew an aide who was looking for work, fluent in Auslan, with two deaf children of her own – one using full Auslan and the other who was implanted and bilingual – the same as Sarah. If the school took her on, Sarah would be able to access the classroom both in English and Auslan.

'This is the aide who would be perfect for Sarah,' I told the assistant principal and handed over her phone number.

In the appeal paper work we sent off on the last day of school, I wrote: 'Sarah's first language is Auslan. The funding level provided will only cover 10 hours of support. What is she supposed to do with the other 15 contact hours at school, let alone during the recess breaks?'

To our surprise, within the first few days of Sarah starting Prep, the Department had upgraded her to Level Three funding, enabling us to get the teacher's aide we'd requested. To my knowledge, Sarah is possibly one of the only children with a cochlear implant in the region with Level Three funding, I think purely because I'd dared to ask for more.

Not only did we succeed in securing the perfect aide for Sarah, as luck would have it, Sarah's teacher turned out to be a former teacher of the deaf! What a joy for her to go from kinder where she'd had no support to a class where both her teacher and her aide were well versed in the education and communication issues encountered by deaf children.

In the classroom, Sarah wore an FM unit and her teacher, a microphone, which when turned on, shut out any background noise, enabling Sarah to hear the teacher's voice without distractions. When the FM unit was turned off, Sarah could once again make herself part of the classroom and all its noisy activity.

In addition, Sarah obtained a visiting teacher of the deaf, who helped her with class work and provided the classroom teacher and the school staff with professional development in the field of hearing loss.

While I was happy that I'd won a small battle, I was still not totally satisfied. Why should a hearing child have 25 hours of access to the curriculum and a deaf child only 10–15? I felt it just wasn't right. I wanted Sarah to have the same opportunities as the other kids.

Our fight for greater access

In July 2006, we approached our local newspaper to write an article about our issue. On 5 July 2006, they published an article entitled 'Department deaf to plea'. In it, I shared the fact that only 10 hours assistance out of 25 contact hours per week was unjust and that I was afraid that my child would fall behind her classmates.

I urged the State Government to increase the funding for Australia's deaf children so that they could have interpreters or technology which allowed for captioning and better trained support staff for all school hours. I also said that the Education Department should provide incentives for teachers to learn sign language and specialist skills for teaching our children with hearing loss. I mentioned that for every child who received disability funding in the school system, there were approximately two that didn't.

I warned the principal that there would be an article in relation to access. I told him that it was not directly against the school, but about the Department of Education's accountability to produce equal learning outcomes for children with a hearing loss to their hearing peers. He understood my frustration and promised he would do the best he could with the resources we had available. It took another two years of active school involvement before we saw any real results.

Doing the research and getting involved

One of the most useful things I have learnt is to do my research and find out what to ask for. As soon as Sarah was diagnosed, I got on the Internet and researched what was out there.

I got myself on the Parents and Friends committee at Monnington because it meant that I developed better working relationships with the professionals working with Sarah and a better insight as to what was going on. Because the teachers knew me, they were more likely to tell me snippets about Sarah and about new developments and new programs for which we could apply.

I am always on the look out for learning tools that will improve Sarah's access to education, flicking through audiovisual catalogues and browsing the Internet to keep abreast of new technology.

When Sarah was in Grade 1, I discovered that, through the Deafness Foundation, she was eligible to apply for funding for an interactive whiteboard. This amazing educational tool has opened up so many opportunities. By being hooked up to the Internet through the teacher's laptop, Sarah is now able to access interactive literacy and numeracy programs.

Shortly after that, I discovered that the Lions Hearing Dogs were donating soundfield amplification systems to children who met the criteria. Immediately, I downloaded the form from the Internet, took it to the principal and said, 'We need to apply for one of these!' The school and Sarah's visiting teacher took the time to write the submission. It was installed at the end of 2007 and the school purchased the microphone to link into it early in 2008.

Upgrading technology

Your child's speech processors, hearing aids and FM units can be upgraded every four to five years through Australian Hearing, depending on their budget, until your child is 21. It is important that the FM unit is upgraded at the same time as the speech processors and/or hearing aids so all your child's technology remains fully compatible. When Sarah's FM unit was ready to be upgraded, her speech processor wasn't, so we held off a little longer and upgraded them together. Sarah's technological needs are all now fully integrated so that the processor and her FM system are now capable of directly connecting to the soundfield amplification system.

Expecting the best of your child

I am a mother of three children – two hearing and one deaf. All my kids are taught the same values. All are expected to be kind, well-mannered and courteous.

The three are expected to give their all to everything and to try their best. I tell them, 'You're not going to get everything right, but you're not going to get everything wrong either. However, if you don't try, you'll get nothing. If you don't try, you'll never know whether you could have got it right or wrong. Just give it your best effort!'

Some people think that my expectations of Sarah are higher than they should be. I expect her to hit every target that other kids would. I want her to be able to achieve everything she can. I want her to have the sense that the only difference with her is that her ears don't function the same way as ours do. That is all.

One day, she sat down at the dining room table, pointed to all of us and said, 'You, you, you and you are different.'

'Oh. Why's that?' I asked.

'Well, I'm deaf so *you're* all different!' she replied.

In Grade 2, Sarah got a teacher who had no experience of deafness so I suspected it was going to be a challenging year. However to the credit of the school, Sarah and the team working with her, Sarah flourished. She soon went from being Level 10 to Level 25 in reading.

Imagine my surprise, joy and pride when Sarah – the only deaf child in a mainstream school – was shortlisted among the eight out of 60 children in her year level for 'Book of the Year', a creative writing program, where every child in the school is expected to write, illustrate and publish their own book on a topic of their choosing.

On the day that the winners were to be announced we waited anxiously at assembly while the Prep and Grade 1 winners, the Grade 2 winners, the third prize winner, then the second accepted their prizes. When Sarah's name wasn't mentioned in any of these categories, I comforted myself that at least she was on par with 50 of her hearing peers in her literacy skills.

Winning 'Book of the Year'

When her name was called out as the first prize winner, Sarah didn't have to have it interpreted for her, she just ran. I am grateful to digital cameras for not needing to use a view-finder; it would have fogged up with all the tears streaming down my face.

How often do you read the words, 'In recognition of your outstanding academic achievement and exceptional performance' on a certificate for a profoundly deaf child in a mainstream school? Almost never, if you believe the negative reports we so often hear and read.

It has been her biggest personal achievement to date. By the end of the Grade 2, she was hitting the highlighted area in which every Grade 2 child should be. Some areas were higher than others, but she was still within the realm of the age-appropriate curriculum.

Sarah has been inspired to achieve. Why strive to survive when you can do so much better? It has only served to reinforce my belief that, with good groundings, anything is possible.

Empowering Sarah and keeping track of her progress

Deaf children will often fall behind their hearing classmates because they don't often understand the spoken concepts. Most hearing kids will say 'Uh huh' to the teacher, still not knowing what they're supposed to be doing, but then will have no trouble gleaning the information from others. Sarah will get visual clues and some of the chatter, but still may be unsure what to do.

She has learnt not to be afraid to ask if she doesn't understand something, or confirm the different tasks she has been asked to do. She's been taught to say, 'I don't understand. Can you say it again?' or 'I still don't understand what you're asking me to do. Can you explain it a different way?'

I'm constantly tracking her progress at school. 'How's she going?' I ask her teachers. 'Is she meeting all the set targets?' If she's not, then I want to know why not. I ask them what I need to do with her to reinforce what they are doing with her so that she will get there. We have regular student support group meetings where we share our opinions on her progress and set out clear goals and strategies for her to achieve the best outcomes.

The team working with Sarah keep a book in her classes and note down any difficulties she is encountering so we can follow those up at home. If they are working on numbers, and if she's setting the table, I ask her, 'How many forks have you got?' or 'How many knives have you got?' If I find an activity at home that would work well for Sarah in the classroom, I share it with her teacher. It's very much a team thing.

I keep a file on Sarah, containing everything from her letter of diagnosis to her latest school reports. When she started kinder and primary school, I took it to the team and said, 'Please photocopy whatever you want out of this file. If you ever read an article of interest in the newspaper, please share it with me. If I see one, I'll share it with you.'

Sarah has to concentrate harder than hearing kids in order to get what they naturally do. Hearing kids don't receive education between 7.30am and 7.30pm, seven days a week, but she does. We have to do spelling and reading and constant language input. She works hard, but she's happy to do it.

> *'To look back at the things she has achieved in such a short time challenges me to look at what I can do to help her achieve even more in the future.'*

Sarah is my inspiration, my driving force. To look back at the things she has achieved in such a short time challenges me to look at what I can do to help her achieve even more in the future. Only last night she sat at the dining table, did her homework, and triumphantly declared, 'I've finished! And you didn't help me.' I am so very proud of her.

Changing the LOTE to Auslan

I urged the school to build a community around Sarah that could communicate with her both orally and in Auslan. When my eldest daughter Emma started school, I asked the principal, 'Can we look at changing the LOTE to Auslan?' He looked at me like I was mad! So I let it go because Sarah wasn't at the school yet.

When Sarah started at the school, I went back to the principal and said, 'Is there any possibility of changing the LOTE to Auslan? It would be wonderful if Sarah's community felt like they were part of why Sarah had an Auslan aide and vice versa.'

Year 1 and 2 kids singing and signing 'What a Wonderful World' at a recent school assembly

This time I got the very political line, 'We have an Italian LOTE teacher on contract. Until she chooses to leave, we will not be able to change it.'

I jokingly replied, 'I'll have to work on her to leave then!' and left.

Eight months later, the principal approached me, saying that the LOTE teacher had decided to go back into a full-time classroom and the school wanted to change the LOTE to Auslan. He wanted to know if they had my support in doing so before they took it to the school council. The decision was accepted unopposed.

I've been blown away by the school's commitment to sign language. It's not only Sarah who is benefitting. The response from students, parents, staff and the community has been one of excitement and enthusiasm. Sarah now feels far more part of the community and her self-esteem has soared.

Sarah now has a fully qualified interpreter for four hours a week and an aide for 10 hours. Her interpreter is there for the whole school assembly not only supporting *her* to access this event, but also the other students who are learning the language. They are getting to see how Auslan works in real life situations.

Dealing with the hard stuff

Some days are hard with Sarah. One day she pointed to her hearing aid in her right ear, and said, 'I don't want to wear this anymore! When I grow up, I won't need it.'

'Well, you'd better give it to me because when I grow up, I probably will,' I replied.

She looked at me puzzled.

'As I get older, my hearing might get worse and I might need your hearing aid. You'd better stick it in a draw now and you can try it again tomorrow.'

'We always try to take the focus off her hearing impairment and make it about who she is as a person.'

Some days she refuses to wear it, so I say, 'If you don't want to wear it, that's fine, then don't, but you have to understand that you won't hear me, music, birds, or anything. Your hearing aid is your friend. Without it, you can't hear. If you want to not hear and use Auslan, that's fine.'

Sarah's greatest challenge as she gets older is social interaction. At times, she'll say, 'My friends won't play with me because I'm different.'

I reply, 'No. Your friends don't want to play with you because they don't want to play the game you're playing. You don't have to be everybody's friend and not everybody's going to be your friend.'

I tell her, 'It's not about what you wear and it's not about what you've got attached to your head. It's about who you are.

The main thing is that you are nice and polite to others even if they aren't nice back to you.'

We always try to take the focus off Sarah's hearing impairment and make it about who she is as a person.

I believe her classmates love her being there. One day she was doing cartwheels on the oval and realised that her hearing aid had come out. It was like Chinese whispers through the school as a search line of kids formed, walking with great purpose across the oval until they found it. When she thanked the little boy who had located it, he simply replied, 'That's alright. You can't hear without it.'

Most importantly, her love of school amazes me every day. When we had to get her new FM unit, I said, 'You can stay home with me for an hour or you can go straight to school,' and she said, 'No Mum, I'm going to school!' She'd go seven days a week if she could! She just loves being part of everything and hates to think she's missing out.

The Deaf community

It's really important for both you and your child to get involved with and learn about deaf people and the Deaf community. I take Sarah to the VicDeaf rallies and other events where she can see deaf adults and know that there is a whole community of people who are like her.

I work at Deaf Children Australia where I can get regular access to deaf adults and young people. I'm always asking them questions about what it was like for them growing up. 'What did your parents do that worked for you as a child?' 'What did your parents do that annoyed you when you were growing up?' 'What is it that bugged you that you couldn't get when you were growing up?' I make note of their answers and try not to make those mistakes with Sarah.

Left to right: John, Jack, Emma, Roz and Sarah

The parents of a deaf friend of mine never learnt to sign. My friend is oral but loves being in the Deaf community because she feels comfortable there. I always keep that in mind. I don't want Sarah to get to the point where she says, 'My mum could never communicate with me.'

My job title at Deaf Children Australia is parent services coordinator. One of my tasks is to run a national parent council which keeps a group of parents from all over Australia informed about what is happening in other states. Each state has both positive and negative policies and services, but it's interesting to compare and contrast them.

Parent mentoring is probably the biggest part of my job at the moment. The Beacon Program, as it is known, links parents of newly diagnosed deaf babies with parents who have walked a similar path before them.

Sarah at a calisthenics competition

I could work at any other job, but then I'd still need to do all my homework for Sarah. This way I get to do both!

Siblings

I recently read a novel called *My Sister's Keeper* by Jodi Picoult which can really make you feel guilty about what you've done to your other kids for the sake of your special needs child.

Initially, Sarah's deafness may have been hard on Emma and Jack. We travelled a lot to Australian Hearing, the Eye and Ear Hospital and the Royal Children's Hospital. I tried to make Emma and Jack understand that this was not because Sarah enjoyed going, but because she had to go.

When they were little, I relied a lot on Emma to be Sarah's ears. My youngest, Jack speaks so well because he got dragged along to all the speech therapy meetings! Now that they are getting older and Sarah is fiercely independent, the others aren't relied upon nearly as much.

I make sure that I give Emma and Jack quality time at every opportunity so that we can do all those things they love to do.

Sarah swimming at school

Sarah's future

So where has that road we began with Sarah at 15½ months old taken us? It's been an unimagined journey – one which we are only part way along, but which has brought many successes. Remember that success is in the eye of the beholder.

At nine years old, Sarah is fluent in two languages – Auslan and English. She already has a literary prize under her belt. She has children requesting to be in her class next year and a great network of friends, both deaf and hearing.

Sarah receiving a 'You Can Do It!' award for being organised!

She's now in Grade 4 at a school that has embraced Sarah's deafness and taken on Auslan as a LOTE for all the children. She has an incredible team working with her – the same aide and visiting teacher as last year, a classroom teacher who has Level One and Two in Auslan and a student support officer, fluent in Auslan, who helps Sarah when needed. Sarah is very happy. She has her soundfield amplification system and her new pink behind-the-ear cochlear implant processor, which she loves. She does swimming lessons and calisthenics.

She'll go to the local secondary school with all the other kids from her local primary school, so she'll have lots of friends. She wants to be a scientist when she's older so she can invent a waterproof implant that doesn't need to be taken off in the pool. 'Or,' she said, 'I could become an interpreter because I already know how to do it. Or I might be a dancer.' I tell her that if she wants something enough and works hard enough like anyone else, she can be whatever she wants to be.

As for driving and getting married, well, what was I thinking? Nothing can stop her now.

Accessing both worlds

Gavin Rose-Mundy works at a signing school for deaf children as a LOTE teacher and senior teacher's assistant. He also teaches Auslan at TAFE and at the Deaf Education Network. Married to Rebekah Rose-Mundy who works as an employment officer at The Deaf Society of NSW, they live in Sydney's Carlingford with three of their four children – Phoenix (four), Scarlett Oceania (15 months) and Archer (four months). The whole family is deaf.

'WOULD PHOENIX BE SUITABLE for a cochlear implant?' I asked the audiologist.

My wife Becky looked at me, stunned. I knew what she was thinking. How could I have asked such a question, given that we were both proudly Deaf*? Neither of us had ever viewed deafness as a disability. Being integral members of the Deaf community, we both cherished the Deaf culture and all its values, which had always played a significant part in our lives.

---

*Please note that we describe ourselves as 'deaf', never 'hearing impaired'. We dislike the term 'hearing impaired'. We find it cold and clinical, and implying a disability. It is also not a word commonly used in deafness circles anymore. 'Hard of hearing' is. Deaf with a capital 'D' is used in reference to deaf culture and identity. Deaf with a small 'd' refers to the physical condition of not hearing. For more on this, please see page 178 under 'Deaf community'.

It made no sense that I would now want to have my first child implanted. I was born deaf into a Deaf family with Auslan as my mother language. I had enjoyed an incredibly happy childhood. I had gone to a deaf school. I had enjoyed the company of Deaf friends and had been able to sign both at school and at home. Surely I should be the last person to consider this new technology that claimed to be a 'cure' for deafness and threatened the future of the Deaf community? Weren't Deaf people supposed to be loyal advocates of 'Deafness'?

'No,' replied the audiologist. 'It is only possible with profound and not moderate hearing loss.'

Becky breathed a sigh of relief. She was all too aware of the potential pain and feelings of isolation that disconnection from the Deaf community could bring a deaf child. Unlike me, Becky had been born profoundly deaf to a hearing family who had taken great pains to ensure that she become part of the hearing world, wear hearing aids and learn to speak and lipread.

But all this had brought her was a despairing sense of not belonging in the hearing world, until at 14, when she'd been introduced to sign language and the Deaf community and had never looked back. Implanting our child, she feared, could potentially destroy the Deaf identity and Deaf values she had grown to love.

But there was method to my apparent 'madness'. While I was grateful for my happy childhood, with age, I had come to see that my exclusion from the hearing world hadn't served me. Our world revolved around, and was so much more accessible for, hearing people and I didn't want my own children to suffer the same frustrating lack of opportunities I'd endured by not being able to speak.

When Phoenix was born deaf, I was initially floored, because I hadn't expected him to be. Becky came from a full hearing family which I believed significantly reduced the likelihood of *our* children being deaf. Then emerged a flood of ambivalent emotions. One part of me felt relief that he was just like me and that we'd be able to share similar experiences. The other part felt pure dread about his future.

What concerned me most was his educational future. My parents, both who had grown up in signing Deaf environments, had sent my brother Shane and me to the very same deaf signing school in Melbourne as my father himself had been educated. All lessons were conducted in sign language and finger spelling. There had been no need to speak.

When I was eight, my family relocated to Sydney, where we were sent to a school for deaf children. All lessons there were conducted in Signed English, an unpleasant method of communication, far slower than Auslan, which I was then forced to learn.

For my parents growing up in the 1940s, oral or bilingual schools hadn't existed as options. So, for them, sending us to signing deaf schools seemed like the logical, natural choice. But there were more options available to us now. I wanted to explore what was out there.

The poor standard of education I had experienced growing up was certainly not what I wanted to inflict on my own children. All around me were examples of Deaf adults who had gone to deaf schools, who had chosen the signing path, had rejected speech, or who had not had the option of learning speech at school, and who could now only read or write very poorly. Too few succeeded in finishing Year 12 and getting through to university.

On the other hand, many of those who I'd seen attend a deaf unit in a hearing school with support from a teacher of the deaf, and had learnt both speech and Signed English exercised far better written and verbal communication skills. As a result, these people now enjoyed increased opportunities in both the deaf and hearing communities.

Whatever differing opinions Becky and I had, we remained strongly aligned on the fact that we would do whatever was necessary to ensure our children received the same opportunities as any hearing child, even if this meant that we would have to adapt our lives a little to fit into the hearing world.

Our own childhoods had been valuable lessons in teaching us what we didn't want for our children. While I had loved being part of the Deaf community, I had disliked being disconnected

> 'While I had loved being part of the Deaf community, I had disliked being disconnected from the hearing community in the same way that Becky had resented being cut off from the Deaf community. We did not want to set the same limitations on our children as had been placed on us.'

from the hearing community in the same way that Becky had resented being cut off from the Deaf community. We did not want to set the same limitations on our children as had been placed on us.

I was also very aware that the Deaf community wasn't as strong as it had been 40 years ago. The majority of deaf children were being born to hearing families who were now choosing to give their children hearing aids or implants and place them in mainstream schools.

Left to right: 17-year-old Heloise holding Archer (nine months), Becky holding Scarlett (two) and Gavin holding Phoenix (four), Canberra

We came to the conclusion that we wanted to expose our children to both sign and spoken language. Why should we set boundaries for them to have only one language if it was going to limit them in later life?

If this meant having to give our children the latest technology such as hearing aids and cochlear implants then so be it. This would give them the option to integrate into the hearing community, while at the same time, allow them to be part of the Deaf community through sign language.

Growing up, I'd felt restricted by not being able to hear or speak. I wished that I'd been encouraged to speak and to hear with the help of hearing aids. Wonderful new technology had been invented, so why couldn't we try it? Rather than viewing this technology as something that threatened deafness, I saw it as a tool that could create flexibility and new opportunities.

Becky had encouraged her first child, Heloise, to sign, be oral and lipread. The results spoke for themselves. Now at 17, Heloise has excellent spoken English, an adequate knowledge of sign language, is top of her English and French class at a hearing school, is doing Year 12 in Canberra and wants to be an English teacher in the near future. Our intention was to do the same for our other kids.

Given that both Becky and I were fluent in Auslan and used it at home to communicate, we weren't so much concerned with our children's ability to pick up sign as much as how they were going to develop their second language, speech.

I realised for my parents it must have been relatively easy, putting me straight into a deaf school and not having to worry about the added pressures of hearing aid appointments, attending speech therapy sessions or looking for bilingual schools.

There was no doubt about it. The route that Becky and I had chosen for our children was going to require a lot more soul searching, perseverance and commitment.

That has proved to be an understatement. It has been a highly challenging path, fraught with controversy and battles along the way.

Our greatest struggle has been to find a school in Sydney that will enable our children to develop both languages. You know that educational choices are severely limited when you can't find a single school in a whole state that uses both speech and sign.

Time and time again we have come up against the negative attitudes of educators who resolutely believe that deaf children born to hearing parents should be oral and attend oral schools, and deaf children born to Deaf parents should be signing and attend deaf signing schools. According to them, teaching both sign and speech at the same time is wrong.

Is it wrong to teach a child English and German at the same time? Why restrict a child to just one language, when two will allow them more freedom and possibilities? These attitudes should be carefully examined if these educators care about the future wellbeing of these children.

It is also well documented that hearing children greatly benefit from learning signs at childcare or pre-school to bridge the communication gaps. Why not apply this same logic to deaf children?

Once Phoenix had been fitted with hearing aids, we spent hours researching early intervention schools and attending

Phoenix, four years old

speech therapy sessions. We also went through training ourselves to ensure he understood the various sounds at home, and Becky read him stories in both speech and sign.

When Phoenix was two, we placed him into a pre-school where the curriculum is taught in Auslan with the aim that the kids become fluent in both English and sign. However, as Auslan was the language we used at home, I asked the teachers to speak as well as sign with him. Hesitant at first, they told me it was not their policy to do both, but later agreed because he was not receiving much English at home.

It didn't take long for us to notice that the signing school did not suit Phoenix at all and he was becoming increasingly frustrated. We suspected this was due to his ability to hear so well, that he did not wish to sign.

When he turned three, we decided to transfer him to an oral pre-school to see if that would make any difference. Unfortunately, the manager of early childhood services in deafness and hearing impairment at the oral school had a hard time accepting that a deaf child who was signing at home would be appropriate for an oral school. He expressed his doubts that my son's speech skills would ever improve. He said he feared that Phoenix would 'influence' other children into using sign language.

'Phoenix should be signing,' he told me outright. I point blank refused to accept this.

'Other children learn two languages at the same time,' I stated. 'Why can't my son learn to speak and sign at the same time? You know that this is not right. You have to offer my child this opportunity.'

In the end, it took eight months of debates that included my threatening to take the school to the discrimination tribunal, before they reluctantly agreed to take my son.

What resulted, when we trialled him at the oral pre-school two days a week and the other two days at the deaf signing school, was nothing short of fascinating. For as long as Phoenix was at the deaf signing school, he ignored teachers when they signed to him and preferred to speak. Being the youngest, he gullibly copied inappropriate behaviour from the badly behaved kids and began to demonstrate behavioural problems.

At the oral school, however, it was a whole different ball game. Instead of his frequent episodes of getting into trouble, he now seemed genuinely enthralled by every word his teacher said. He devoured all work tasks, played respectfully with the other kids and returned home happy at the end of each school day.

As his behaviour at the signing school grew more wild, we decided that it simply wasn't working for him and transferred him to the oral pre-school five days a week.

Since then, not only have his speaking skills gone through the roof, but his English vocabulary has expanded to the point where he is outperforming the other kids in his class. As an added bonus, his Auslan, which we still use with him everyday, has also dramatically improved.

I think we have definitely made the right choice for Phoenix. Our ultimate goal for him would be to put him in a mainstream public school with the support of an interpreter. But we are still struggling to find one in which to enrol him, and we continue to hit brick walls when it comes to finding bilingual- and deaf-friendly programs. It is quite obvious that attitudes need to change vis-à-vis the bilingual approach to deafness in the educational sector and in the wider community.

It is also clear that the government needs to commit more money to support deaf kids in mainstream schools. It costs schools around $40,000 a year to employ a sign language interpreter. Yet most deaf children receive only a small portion of this in government funding. Where is the rest going to come from?

There are just under 900 teachers of the deaf for approximately 16,000 deaf kids across Australia. Many of these seem to be oral and not signing. Teachers of the deaf need to be able to have the appropriate signing skills and an adequate understanding of Deaf culture.

Scarlett Oceania and the cochlear implant

When our little girl Scarlett Oceania was born on 12 April 2006, Becky knew instinctively that she was deaf. The chart at the audiologist's flat-lined, indicating a 120 decibel loss which meant that she was profoundly deaf. The second time around, discovering our child was deaf was much easier to take.

That day, I decided to research everything I could about cochlear implants. When I mentioned this to my wife, however, she was devastated. Her moist blue eyes told me that she was thinking, 'Who are you? You are not the proud Deaf man I married.'

Isn't it ironic? If you'd asked me if I would have considered a cochlear implant 10 years ago, I would have been vehemently opposed to the idea and the answer would have been a very definite NO! But opinions can change with life experience. After having spent six years working with deaf children, my attitude to the implant certainly had.

Having worked with many deaf children with implants, I saw the benefits that cochlears provided them: the joy at now being able to communicate with their families at home, participate in games with other kids and listen to music.

'Please can we just give it six months, do a bit of research and explore the possibility before we say no to an implant?' I begged Becky. I didn't think we understood enough about them to rule them out completely.

'Fine,' she agreed reluctantly after many hours of debate. 'Just six months.'

I was grateful for some time to be able to decide on the right way to go for our daughter. But my heart was heavy. I knew that Becky was only doing her best to respect the fact that Scarlett was also *my* daughter and that I was entitled to have some input as to how we brought her up. Inside though, I knew she was adamant that she did not want to have Scarlett implanted.

When Scarlett was five weeks old, we set up a meeting with the ENT surgeon to discuss whether she was even eligible for the implant. He told us that she would require MRIs, CAT scans and various electrode tests to check her decibel loss and that it would be another few months before she could be operated on.

The tests later showed she had a 115 decibel loss in her right ear and total loss in her left. We were told that it made no difference as to which of her ears was implanted; we could in fact choose.

In the six months that followed, I rolled up my sleeves and launched into researching everything I could about the cochlear. Becky and I attended meetings and discussions, and engaged in countless debates about the positive and negative impact of the implant on Scarlett's life and on those around her.

In the meantime, we had her fitted with hearing aids when she was barely eight weeks old. There was no response to sound at all, even when drums were beaten close to her. This gave me even more incentive to have her implanted.

I'll make no secret about the fact that making the decision to implant Scarlett was one of the most difficult we have ever had to make. One reason was that we were well known and highly regarded in the Deaf community. Given that we were going to be one of the first Deaf families to implant our deaf child, this decision was inevitably going to cause waves.

On breaking our news to the Deaf community, we were pleasantly surprised by the way in which most of the members responded. 'This is your child and ultimately your decision,' they said. 'We respect whatever path you decide to take.' A few even praised us for having the courage to step outside the box and take this leap.

However, as predicted, a few openly expressed their aversion to our groundbreaking decision. 'How could you do such a thing? You come from a Deaf family!' some argued. 'Why are you trying to change your identity?' questioned others. I tackled each question as diplomatically as I could.

'Did you know that they drill into the head?' someone asked me one day, with wide eyes.

'It's only a little incision. It's not a huge drill,' I replied without faltering.

Two little holes are drilled into the skull, one for optical viewing, the other for the implant electrodes to get through to the cochlear. The processor would be embedded into the skull, which, if two nerves were accidentally struck, could cause face paralysis or loss of taste ability. But the risk of this ever occurring was close to minimal. The last mishap had occurred six years ago. Surgeons now possessed far superior equipment to monitor and detect the correct nerve, and electrodes could be inserted with minimum risk. The chance that my daughter would hear was far greater.

I felt like I was in the firing line, but inside I was determined not to care what others thought. It was our decision and I knew in my heart why I wanted this for our daughter. As far as I was concerned, it was just like getting a hearing aid, only far more powerful.

I knew with time the majority of the Deaf community would respect our decision, whatever that ended up being. It was the 20%, who were heavily involved in Deaf politics, getting their backs up about something they perceived as a massive threat to the sustainability of their community. But things were changing.

Having to share our decision with my extended family proved to be even more difficult. While they all expressed their dismay that we could even contemplate such a thing, it was my hearing sister who appeared most upset.

Writing from London, where she worked as a British sign language interpreter in Deaf TV productions, she asked, 'Why did you come to this decision? What happened to Deaf values that you have been preaching about? Does this mean that you have turned your back on the Deaf community?'

My sister had been the only hearing one in our deaf family and like us, had grown up in a signing environment with Auslan as her mother language. She later learnt to speak English and is now fluent in both languages.

She'd seen her two older brothers who are very Deaf in their values and identity and enjoyed being part of one of the most proudly Deaf families in Deaf society. She had also worked as an interpreter with many Deaf people.

Her comments hurt and she succeeded in swaying my position for a moment. Yet I was quick to remind her that the decision ultimately lay with Becky and me as to what steps we took for our daughter's future.

'It is all well and good to preach about what idealistically seems right, but you won't have to pick up the pieces when she is struggling at school because she can't hear,' I pointed out.

Eventually my whole family accepted our decision.

Ironically, one of my sister's friends, a successful interpreter who himself had Deaf parents, made the comment: 'So Scarlett will be the same as your sister and myself!'

'No, she will not be the same as either of you,' I replied. 'Scarlett having an implant does not mean she will be 'hearing'. She will always be deaf. However, we are hoping that she will have something in common with you both by having the ability to converse in two languages.'

He apologised for not thinking. While I was not offended, his attitude highlighted the belief shared by many deaf and hearing people that having an implant cures deafness and turns them into a hearing person.

Becky made the choice not to involve her family because they were hearing and she felt that they had never really taken her identity as a Deaf person seriously. Dragging them into it, she believed, might cause her to stray from her own inner knowing. She didn't want to be swayed by judgements foreign to her own.

What kept us going was Becky's and my desire to give Scarlett whatever we could to increase her opportunities to be fluent in sign and spoken English. We could have waited until she was older and allowed her to make her own decision, but by then, the crucial language developmental stage would have passed. It would have been too late.

By the end of six months (which felt more like 20 years!) of countless conversations with doctors who patiently explained to us all the pros and cons, Becky became more and more convinced about the benefits of having an implant and I was more confident than ever that the operation was the right thing to do.

We did not want Scarlett turning to us when she was older and saying, 'Mum and Dad, why did you deprive me of the opportunity to hear and speak? Why did you limit my ability to communicate?' We wanted a girl who was self-assured, confident in her ability to cross over from one world to another; someone who was able to socialise with both hearing and deaf friends.

In November 2006 when Scarlett was seven months old, she went in for an implant in her right ear because we felt it would better respond. The weeks leading up to it were an agony. Although Becky was now comfortable with our decision, she kept getting cold feet and wanting to back out.

Her greatest concern was that, with the cochlear, Scarlett would lose her Deaf identity. She was also very worried about the backlash of the Deaf community and our reputation being permanently damaged as a result of doing what we were doing.

She knew that she could cancel the whole operation right up until the day of surgery if she wanted to. A few days prior to surgery, she was on the verge of calling the whole thing off.

It was an agonising time. While I wanted to go ahead with it, I became increasingly anxious about the surgical procedure and what could potentially go wrong – brain damage, facial paralysis, the side effects of the anaesthetic, the list went on. While the thoughts of all the risks consumed me, Becky feared more that the implant might fail, that Scarlett would go through all that pain and end up hearing nothing.

On the way to the hospital, the car was deathly silent. My anxiety levels became unbearable.

All of a sudden Becky said, 'I don't care what other people say. This is the right thing to do.'

Her words should have been a comfort. Instead they threw me into the most horrible doubt.

When the nurses took Scarlett to the preparation room and put the gas mark on her tiny face, I looked on helplessly. When they asked me to stay outside, I descended into panic – a paralysis of frightening thoughts and feelings that lasted for the next few hours.

What had possessed us to do this?

Was this the right thing for our little girl?

What would happen if the operation failed?

Despite the surgeons' repeated assurances that it was a major, but uncomplicated procedure, I simply couldn't escape the nagging fear that Scarlett's brain might be damaged from the surgery.

Three excruciating hours later, the surgeon emerged with a broad smile.

'The operation was a great success. Your daughter can hear!'

I couldn't believe it. I felt pure elation that the surgery had gone well and dumbfounded that she was now able to hear.

Over the course of the next three weeks, they began the gradual process of 'switching her on' – moving first from 10 electrodes to 16 then finally to 22. All at once would have been too overwhelming for her.

Then the miracle happened. Someone in the room laughed and Scarlett did too. Hearing the laughter had set off her own fit of giggles. I was excited and intrigued.

It's been almost two years since Scarlett had her implant and she is doing so well with sounds; I am continually amazed at how much she hears.

One afternoon, just before she turned two, she came and told me that the baby upstairs was crying. I glanced at the baby alarm but it wasn't flashing. I asked Phoenix if this was true. He shook his head and signed 'no'. Scarlett was unyielding. On climbing the staircase, Phoenix suddenly signed, 'Yes, Daddy. It's true! The baby *is* crying!' Scarlett must hear even better than Phoenix with his moderate loss and hearing aids.

At just two years old, our little girl is fluent in sign language, knows the difference between sounds and is improving in her speech at a rapid rate. With access to both worlds, she moves with ease between sound and sign, communicating with both the hearing and the deaf. It is a joy to watch.

At the moment, she is unable to distinguish between who is deaf and who is hearing, but this will unfold naturally as she gets older. Despite the Sydney Cochlear Implant Centre offering to implant Scarlett's other ear free of charge, we have decided to leave this decision up to her.

Scarlett enjoying her second birthday present

A few people who have had two implants have told me that having two made perhaps a 10% improvement in their hearing. One boy even expressed his regret about having the second one. He said it would have had the same effect to simply turn his head slightly to catch sounds from the other side of his head. Some hearing parents have told me that a second implant is not as effective as the first one. This made it easy not to proceed with the second implant.

Scarlett had to attend a number of therapy appointments at the Cochlear Implant Centre and the Welywn Centre so that she would learn to hear and speak with her new implant. During the speech training, Becky and I were encouraged to speak with her as much as possible.

Originally both centres requested that the interpreter hide behind Scarlett so that Scarlett couldn't see her, but we refused to permit this. Bilingualism involves both languages. It felt deceitful to be concealing Scarlett's mother language from her. We resolved this by getting the interpreter to sit beside her so she was still in her line of sight, but was not the centre of attention.

She now attends the Roberta Reid Pre-school where her teachers are happy to use both speech and sign language. We feel we are making progress with creating the possibility of a bilingual world for other children. It is interesting that while Phoenix was frustrated at signing school, Scarlett loves every minute of it.

It has taken some time for Becky to totally accept the implant, but she is now happy with her decision. She has told me that she worries sometimes that one day when Scarlett is older, she will say, 'Mummy, Daddy, why did you give me an implant? Why did you try to change me? What's wrong with being deaf?' While this may or may not happen, I feel confident that Scarlett will appreciate being able to select the world she wants for herself rather than being constrained to just one.

Scarlett at her second birthday

It means a lot to Becky that Scarlett develops a strong Deaf identity and that the Deaf community do not treat her any differently for having an implant. Attitudes in the Deaf community seem to be naturally transforming as more and more people are making the decision

125

to be implanted and more and more are making the choice for two languages and two worlds.

While Scarlett's implant has had little impact upon the way our family communicates, Scarlett and Phoenix are very different in each of their communication needs.

Scarlett loves her implant and forever wears it on her head, well aware that it brings her the gift of sound. Yet in her speech, her body language and her strong use of signs, she has a 'Deaf aura', expressing herself more like a 'Deaf person'. Naturally preferring the signing environment and the company of Deaf people, she seems proud and empowered to be Deaf.

Ironically, a few weeks ago, a Deaf lady who had fervently opposed our decision to implant Scarlett, sat opposite Scarlett at a function and began to sign with her. 'She is beautiful!' she signed to her friend. 'She is so Deaf!' Then she noticed me looking at her. Her eyes widened as she realised who it was. Turning back to Scarlett, she saw the processor and coil on her head. The penny dropped. This was indeed 'the Deaf girl with the cochlear implant'.

'You are right,' I replied, 'She is very Deaf'. It was a moment of pride and victory for me.

Phoenix, on the other hand, is 'hearing'. While he accepts signing, he prefers to express himself with his voice. Being a naturally inquisitive little boy, he asks frequent questions. While other signing deaf kids

Signing to her brother to 'shush'!

tend to use lots of facial expressions, Phoenix uses few. He signs with our family only because we sign with him. If we sign with him too much, he'll simply look away until we start speaking.

He'll even yell, 'Dad!' at me and when I reply, 'Don't yell, please! I'm deaf. Just tap me!' he says, 'Oh, right, I forgot!'

Archer

When our third baby Archer was born hearing, I almost had a heart attack. I admit I had become a bit complacent about having another deaf child. It took a few days for me to get used to the prospect. After that I worried that he would feel left out being the only 'hearing' one in our family so I went out of my way not to treat him any differently from the others.

Scarlett (22 months), Archer (two months) and Phoenix (three and a half)

Despite it being confirmed through an audiology test at six weeks old that he was hearing, in the coming months, we began to suspect that he was experiencing difficulties hearing us.

When he was seven months old, we had him retested. Again we were assured that apart from a glue blockage in both ears, his hearing was normal. Doubtful that this was the case, we requested to see the reports only to discover that the two tests clearly showed concerns about his ability to hear well. Why was this being hidden from us? Surely we as parents were entitled to get accurate information first-hand?

After treatment with antibiotics for the glue blockage yielded no success, we demanded a third test when Archer was 10 months old. This one indicated that he had a mild hearing loss.

Becky and I have had mixed feelings about this. It has certainly raised a number of questions. What does 'mild hearing loss' mean? Will he be regarded as 'deaf' or 'hearing'? How much has he missed out on in his first 10 months? Will he identify himself as 'deaf' because his family are all deaf? Will he be eligible for trained speech therapy, oralism programs, government financial support, deaf school and university or will he be considered not deaf enough? We are aware that some organisations will only support children who have a 50 decibel or greater hearing loss. Will we need to fight for him to gain access to deaf services? Will he be able to play for his state in the Australian Deaf Games or Deaflympics? These are the new challenges facing Becky and me.

Raising deaf children

I do not like to offer any advice about what to do with your child. Children all have different needs. My kids are testament to that. Just believe in yourself and be open to exploring every avenue to achieve the best for your child.

It is not wise to set any limitations on them just because they are deaf. I can assure you, they are perfect human beings who can do anything they want with the right support and if they put their heart and mind to it.

I believe that the most important qualities to bring into a home with a deaf child are love, regular communication and integration. Show your kids that you are proud of them and that they bring you much joy. This will bring out the best in them.

Be open-minded with your child about their deafness. Let them explore their Deaf identity by mixing with other deaf children and deaf adults and reading about Deaf culture. Celebrating their deafness will allow them to celebrate who they are, increase their confidence, and allow them to bask in the best of both worlds.

'Celebrating their deafness will allow them to celebrate who they are, increase their confidence, and allow them to bask in the best of both worlds.'

I believe that Auslan must be a strong component in the home. While my wife can speak very well, we are unwavering about using Auslan at home. The kids know that if they speak, they must use sign language alongside their words.

We make sure we communicate with our children as much as possible. We don't exclude any of them from family conversations. This works in the same way as it does for hearing children who absorb spoken language from their parents during discussions at dinner time.

When conversing, we go down to our children's eye level so that they feel more comfortable when expressing themselves, instead of having to look up at us, while we stand. Sometimes it would be so much easier simply signing to our kids instead of having to speak to them. But we remind ourselves of why we are doing it and the opportunities we are giving them. It makes it all worthwhile.

Even if your child has a cochlear implant, there is value in teaching your child Auslan, because they still need to be able to communicate when they are not wearing the implant. Implants do not cure deafness. Giving your child access to both hearing and deaf worlds will ensure that your child is not limited to just one.

When Phoenix and Scarlett were babies, I took them to an early intervention program where I met 15 other parents of deaf babies. All had opted for spoken language with their children and had no intention of allowing them to learn sign.

Some even mentioned they had been advised not to teach their baby sign language by doctors and educators. I find it shocking and disappointing that so-called professionals are so biased. They should be advising parents to be open-minded and explore every opportunity to encourage communication in their children.

Some months later, two of these parents changed their mind and began trying out both languages when their children had failed to improve with only spoken language. What a blessing this is for these children. By the time they are two or three, they will still be young enough to grasp language quicker than those who are leaving sign for later or not at all.

I liken the concept of your child having two languages to a tightrope with a safety net underneath. When your child falls off the tightrope with one language, they have the other as a safety net. With only one language, however, without the comfort of a second language, they will fall into the void of no language and suffer.

Hearing parents need to keep an open mind about giving their child access to both worlds as early as possible. The essentials of language are in place by the age of seven. It is far too late to begin teaching your child Auslan at 10 years or older.

If deaf children are not exposed to an effective system of language early on, they run the risk of being seriously and permanently 'disabled' in their lives. To be deprived of language, to not be able to communicate with other human beings leads to the most dire feelings of isolation and worse.

Two years ago, I taught a 14 year old, whose language level was that of a five year old, to sign for the first time in his life. With minimal signing skills, he was barely able to talk. This is a crime! If he'd been taught to sign and speak when he was a baby, his language would now be relatively advanced and he would be enjoying a 'normal' life.

Fortunately, he was hungry to learn and was able to pick up signing fairly quickly. Now at 16, he has developed the language skills of a 14 year old and speaks and signs more confidently than ever before.

Parents need to encourage understanding in their deaf child at all costs. I spend two hours with my deaf students each day reading and writing from English to Auslan and back. I explain things over and over until they understand every word.

'My ultimate goal would be to see deaf children on a par with hearing children in their literacy and language levels.'

Within eight to nine weeks, these students progress from having great difficulty reading and not particularly enjoying it to reading and understanding every word and loving it. My ultimate goal would be to see deaf children on a par with hearing children in their literacy and language levels.

Encourage your child to practise their speech, even if they don't want to. Persevere and they will slowly learn its value. When I was taught to speak as a child, I thought it was a waste of time. Both the school and my parents let me give up without the slightest struggle. Now I wish they'd persisted with me. The potential of deaf children is underestimated in education. Deaf children should be pushed more because they are very capable of achieving.

Becky and I hope that our decisions with our children will succeed in breaking down barriers between the hearing and the deaf communities. We hope that both deaf and hearing parents will see the value in offering both worlds to their deaf children, because it is an asset for their deaf child to have both. Being able to move from one world to another – without limitation – will bring them a level of confidence that would otherwise be lacking.

Things will never change if the Deaf community continues to complain that medical and other professionals do not understand our Deaf world, culture, identity and values. If the hearing world is ever going to 'get' us, we as Deaf people need to start better communicating our needs and working in cooperation with the hearing world to ensure that they do.

By sharing what we are about with the medical professionals and others dealing with our children, we can build connections between the groups, which will promote understanding and build better futures for our children.

Bringing up three deaf kids and one with mild hearing loss, while ourselves being deaf, has presented its own particular set of challenges. But we have always considered ourselves a 'normal' family with our normal share of ups and downs.

I am so grateful to Becky for being there. We have shared the workload and implemented a series of routines which work well for the kids. We are grateful for the support of our family and friends, the Royal Institute of Deaf and Blind Children and its branches and the Sydney Cochlear Implant Centre. We count our blessings every day for having such amazing and beautiful children.

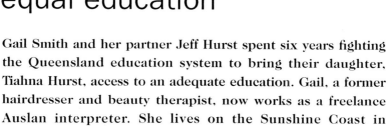

My fight to give my daughter access to an equal education

8

Gail Smith and her partner Jeff Hurst spent six years fighting the Queensland education system to bring their daughter, Tiahna Hurst, access to an adequate education. Gail, a former hairdresser and beauty therapist, now works as a freelance Auslan interpreter. She lives on the Sunshine Coast in Queensland with Jeff, Tiahna (10) and Jacobi (seven).

I GUESS WE WERE LUCKY. When my first child Tiahna was confirmed profoundly deaf two weeks after her birth on 24 February 1998, it came as no surprise. Having two profoundly deaf parents and 22 deaf family members, I didn't go through the 'Why did this happen to me?' and the grief, denial and anger stages that most other hearing parents go through. We just got on with it.

Soon after the diagnosis, we had Tiahna fitted with hearing aids and communicated with her in Auslan, which was to become her first language. All the research we read said that deaf children needed to have a base language to be able to understand language. Considering that Tiahna could not hear

English, we decided to make Auslan her base language from which we would teach her English.

I was already fluent in Auslan having learnt it through my parents who used Auslan rather than speech to communicate. Jeff had to learn it from scratch. We also worked on Tiahna's residual hearing and tried to develop her speech.

I knew that much of the groundwork needed to be done while she was very young. So I began looking around for education options. What I discovered dumbfounded me.

I wanted Tiahna to attend a mainstream school where she would learn alongside deaf and hearing children with the support of a full-time Auslan interpreter. Instead we were advised to send her to a special school. There Tiahna would become the only deaf child in a class full of special needs children under a teacher who could not keep up with Tiahna's fluency in sign language. I was adamant that this was not a suitable option. She was of normal intelligence. She just couldn't hear!

In 1999 I met with the Education Department and requested that Tiahna be moved to a regular school with a sign language interpreter. They told me in no uncertain terms that it was against the education policy in Queensland to be taught in Auslan. I did not find the Department helpful, nor did they seem very interested in Tiahna's case. I knew this was going to be a huge challenge.

Auslan was not being used in Queensland at that time, despite it being the national sign language and the sign language used by the Deaf community. Instead Signed English was the preferred language of instruction, having been introduced into the education system in the 1970s to try and improve the literacy, communication and reading skills of deaf children.

It is vastly inferior to Auslan. Based on spoken English, it has a limited vocabulary, visual inaccuracy and the potential to cause confusion when conveying meaning.

The philosophy had shifted in the last decade to a bilingual-bicultural approach that promoted Auslan as the first language of the deaf. In line with this, other Australian states were phasing out Signed English in favour of Auslan. Despite this, Queensland continued to use Signed English.

Tiahna with her grandmother who is deaf

Above all, Signed English was useless to Tiahna. Auslan was her primary language. I wanted her to use Auslan so that she could communicate with the Deaf community in which she would be involved. Signed English was not recognised as a language in that community. If she went through her schooling in Signed English and later wanted to go to university or TAFE and required an interpreter, there are no interpreters who signed in Signed English, only Auslan. I certainly didn't want a dead end street for my child.

Tiahna had an equal right, as hearing children do, to an equal education and equal information in the classroom. She was entitled to a full-time Auslan interpreter so that she could receive equal access to information at all times.

Up until she started school, Tiahna attended a special education development unit between 1999 and mid-2001, a special education development centre until early 2002, then a state pre-school. During this time, all lessons were conducted in poor attempts at Signed English and not Auslan.

To ensure that she did not fall behind, I stayed and interpreted for her in Auslan. In addition, we spent hours working one on one with her at home and drove each week to Brisbane so that she could have private speech therapy sessions at $65 per hour.

In February 2000, after repeated attempts to negotiate with the Education Department to provide Tiahna with Auslan support in the classroom, I thought, 'This is ridiculous. Full-time Auslan interpreters are being offered to deaf children in other states. Why not in Queensland?' I decided to take the Department to court.

I approached the Queensland Deaf Society in Brisbane to ask for help and was put in touch with a lawyer, Gary Scott, who had deaf parents and a wealth of experience in deafness. Another family, the Jacobs*, were experiencing similar challenges with their deaf child in the Queensland education system so we decided to join our legal actions.

Helen and Tim Jacobs were the hearing parents of 10-year-old Sam who was profoundly deaf. The family did not know Auslan. Sam had been educated first orally and then in Signed English. He was in Grade 6 at a state primary school on the Sunshine Coast. Both parents were hugely concerned about their son's delayed speech, poor language and academic abilities and believed this was largely because he had been deprived of the support he needed to access education. The fact was Sam could barely communicate and had the academic abilities of a five year old.

On 30 May 2002, our families lodged a disability discrimination claim in the Federal Court against Education Queensland.

*The names of this family have been changed at their request to protect their privacy.

Quitting my job to interpret for my daughter

By January 2004, Tiahna, now five, was due to embark on her school career without an interpreter. Just before going into Grade 1 at a primary school on the Sunshine Coast, I approached the principal, informing him that Tiahna desperately needed an interpreter. Our meeting yielded no success.

In the first week of Tiahna starting Grade 1, her teacher pulled me aside and said, 'Tiahna's really struggling. She's not understanding what I'm saying.'

'Yes!' I said, frustrated. 'It's because she's deaf! She desperately needs an interpreter. Please go and tell the principal what you have noticed and ask him to make a recommendation that Tiahna gets a full-time interpreter.'

A few weeks later, the school provided Tiahna with five hours a week of support from an interpreter who was permitted to sign to Tiahna only in Signed English. The interpreter was from Melbourne. Her parents were both deaf. Auslan was her first language. How was it possible that Auslan was both Tiahna's first language and that of the interpreter, yet neither of them was allowed to use it because of Queensland's current education policy? What would it matter to anybody else in the classroom? It was insane!

Five hours of Signed English for a 25 hour week when Tiahna's primary language was Auslan simply wasn't good enough. I needed things to change. So I called the media. Channel Seven and 10, *A Current Affair, The Courier Mail* and our local newspaper jumped on our story.

Responding to my complaints in the media, the Education Department increased Tiahna's hours to 10 hours per week. But what were two hours per day of Signed English going to do for Tiahna?

By February 2004, after countless discussions with the Education Department, Tiahna was given 12.5 hours of Signed English. The hours were all lumped together for the morning sessions from Monday to Thursday. She had no interpreter after lunch from Monday to Thursday or the whole day on Fridays.

What was she going to do for the rest of the time? Lessons were meaningless without an interpreter! I was tired of seeing her coming home upset because she didn't understand what was being talked about in the classroom. She was losing all her confidence and it was breaking my heart. I felt that not giving her adequate support was plain cruel. I wasn't going to let her fall behind. If they weren't going to provide a full-time interpreter, I would have to do it myself.

So that month I quit my job as a hairdresser to act as Tiahna's interpreter for the remaining time she had without one. For six months, I sat alongside her in the classroom. The school policy welcomed parents helping out in the classroom. They didn't stipulate *how many* hours, so when Tiahna didn't have an interpreter, I simply stayed.

On one occasion, the principal told me that this couldn't go on, but I replied, 'That's fine. I'm happy to leave if you get an interpreter to help my daughter. But I'm not leaving until she has one.'

Hurst and Jacobs versus Education Queensland

On 29 March 2004, we fronted the Federal Court in Brisbane for the start of a seven-day hearing after battling the system for almost three years. I didn't want to go to court, but there seemed no other alternative.

Both our families were suing the Queensland State Government for failing to provide an adequate education for our children. The claim stated that because of the inadequate education, their literacy and numeracy had suffered, which would continue into the future, lessening their likelihood of being able to study beyond primary school and affecting their future employability.

The Jacobs family was seeking remedial education and a full-time Auslan interpreter for their son. Our family was seeking a full-time Auslan interpreter for Tiahna and was urging the government to teach the nationally recognised Auslan sign language system.

Both Jeff and I were adamant that we did not want to sue for money. I didn't want a cent. Any money that was made was to be given to the school to help Tiahna. Everyone in Coolum knew me as 'the blonde hairdresser with the little deaf girl'. I didn't want people labelling me as 'the blonde hairdresser with the little deaf girl, who sued and got paid out'.

The case was a landmark one which would have far reaching ramifications for the way the deaf would be taught throughout Australia. One of the main issues was whether deaf children should be taught in Auslan or Signed English.

In his opening address to the court, our counsel James Gray told how 10-year-old Sam had normal intellectual abilities but the education system had so failed him that he had reached the academic standards of a five or six year old.

'The education outcomes for deaf and hearing impaired children are less than they should be,' said Keri Gilbert, the regional services manager of Queensland Deaf Society, outside court that day. 'We would like the government to listen to parents.'

The next morning, the case was plastered across media throughout Australia. 'Deaf kids in test case' read page eight of *The Australian*, 'Parents fight for rights of their deaf children' read page seven of *The Courier Mail*, 'Parents suing' read page six of *The Canberra Times*, 'Govt sued over Coast deaf kids' read the front page of *The Sunshine Coast Daily*. I couldn't believe this was happening to us.

On 31 March 2004, giving evidence against the Queensland Government, leading deafness literacy expert, Linda Komasaroff, told the court that the system of Signed English being taught in Australian schools was 'impoverished'. She said that the literacy of Australian deaf children was declining by half a grade a year and that teaching accuracy had dropped to 8% in Australian primary schools.

She said that Auslan was the better option for deaf children because it was used by the Australian Deaf community while Signed English wasn't. She referred to the success of Sweden and Canada where the deaf sign language system had enhanced literacy levels. She told the court that Queensland's schools were deliberately obstructing parents who were keen to adopt Auslan.

I thought that we were making good progress. But luck was not on our side. At the end of the first week, the judge revealed that one of his personal friends worked in the field of deafness and he felt this may bias the whole proceedings. While I desperately wanted to continue, I was well aware of the harm this relationship could do to our case. When the judge asked whether we wanted him to proceed or stand down, we made the decision to start all over again rather than risking not getting a fair trial. Our case was aborted.

By this stage, I was over it. Our fight had been going on for three years yet we hadn't even started the court case.

On Monday 7 June 2004, the case resumed in Brisbane's Federal Court.

The Courier Mail ran an article the following day entitled 'Silence ends as court hears story' showing photos of Jeff and me walking into court. 'A landmark case of two deaf children taking on the Queensland Government ... is back in Court' read the first line of an article in *The Sunshine Coast Daily* on 8 June. '... parents are at the centre of a battle for more funding in state schools for deaf children ...' it went on. It made me feel sick with nerves.

All I wanted was an equal education for my daughter and this whole thing to end.

Justice Bruce Lander listened as he was told how Sam was left with 'cognitive damage and language skills so poor he was unable to tell a simple story'. Our counsel explained this was because he had often sat in class without an interpreter and without the support of Auslan because it was not the policy in Queensland. Sam was attending a state school, but was placed in a special education class despite a normal IQ. He was permitted to join the mainstream class for less challenging subjects but without an interpreter, meaning that he did not receive the same education as his peers.

Our counsel explained that while Tiahna was younger and had therefore not suffered as much damage as Sam, she most definitely would if she did not receive the 'proper instruction.' Our counsel stated that Tiahna had not suffered as much as Sam because I had been interpreting for her in the classroom, for which I had had to give up my job. Despite numerous discussions, Tiahna had only been given 12.5 hours of access, while Sam was only given five.

During the case, Education Queensland disagreed that Auslan was the only appropriate method of communication for teaching deaf children. It denied allegations that its schools did not offer Auslan and that Auslan was never offered to our families. It also stressed that it was due to other reasons and certainly not to the education system that Tiahna and Sam had fallen behind.

In court on 30 June 2004, the counsel for Education Queensland asserted that Signed English met the needs of deaf children and questioned the need for full-time Auslan interpreters for Sam and Tiahna. Their counsel also said that it would be a mistake to bring Auslan into a classroom because it was a totally different language and that it could damage Sam even more if his whole education was conducted in Auslan.

The counsel for Education Queensland brought forward a letter from a speech pathologist to support this contention. It argued that educating Sam in Auslan would be bringing a third language into his education which may not be beneficial.

Our counsel James Gray refuted this by saying, 'Signed English delivers a diminished outcome for children with severe or profound deafness.' This prompted them to bring up Tiahna's excellent language ability, throwing into doubt any allegations of discrimination.

James Gray responded by saying it was about finding a suitable option that best allowed Tiahna to fulfil her future potential.

The court case lasted two weeks. I honestly don't know how I got through it. There were days when I couldn't get out of bed. I'd take the kids to school then come home and collapse. I cried all the time because I felt that the court did not understand the issues and they gave me no time to explain.

I recall one particularly distressing meeting with the Education Department in July, where I'd sat up for four nights beforehand gathering information from all over Australia to show them that Auslan was proven to work and that I was not some mad mother making it all up. But they simply refused to look at it. In the end, I got up from my chair, ran out of the building and stood in the middle of the road, hoping that a truck would hit me. I was so distressed, I couldn't think straight. I was taken to the psychiatric ward at the hospital, where they did a full assessment. I was diagnosed with post-traumatic stress disorder. That's how bad it got.

There were times when I wanted to walk away from the whole situation. Sometimes I would say to my solicitor, 'I can't deal with this anymore. I'm giving up.' What kept me hanging in there was that I loved Tiahna so much.

'What kept me hanging in there was that I loved Tiahna so much.'

A new school

Relations with the school became strained during the Federal Court proceedings to the point where the school decided that I could no longer interpret for Tiahna. This meant that Tiahna was now deprived of the 10 hours of support that I had provided for her.

Because of this, she spent the rest of the semester struggling to follow what was going on in class. During this time, she became so frustrated and depressed that half-way through the year, I took her out of the state school to home-school her.

The school principal made a complaint to the police that I had not sent Tiahna to school. Coming to our home, the police threatened to take her from me because of allegations

I was neglecting her by not sending her to school. No action was taken and I home-schooled her for the rest of the year.

In the long term, the home-schooling program suited neither Tiahna nor me. Despite having social contact with other home-schooled families, Tiahna desperately missed the face-to-face interaction and began to demonstrate behavioural problems. From my side, the court case had taken its toll and I found it difficult teaching her anything when I was so depressed and often crying.

It couldn't go on like this. We decided to enrol her back into school. After being rejected by 14 private schools, Tiahna was finally enrolled at a community college. Before we enrolled her, I told the principal about the court case, the accusations, everything. I wanted him to know before he found out through the grapevine anyway. He was a lovely man – understanding and compassionate. The school fees were expensive but he allowed me to go into Tiahna's classroom every day to interpret for her. Tiahna went there for six months until the outcome of the court case.

Court case lost

On 15 April 2005, our five-year legal battle with the Education Department came to an end. The judge ruled in favour of the Jacob's case and against ours.

The judge, Justice Bruce Lander, found that the Queensland Government had discriminated against Sam because he had not been provided with an Auslan interpreter in the classroom. However, he was reluctant to order Education Queensland to provide Sam with a full-time Auslan interpreter as he felt it was not the court's role to tell educators what to do as they would surely do what was best for the child.

He dismissed Tiahna's case on the basis of 'no discrimination' because he said she had good English skills and in all skill areas was on a par with her hearing peers. She had been able to 'cope' with being educated in English and Signed English (and without Auslan) in the classroom. While he agreed that she would have benefitted from being taught in Auslan, she had not suffered any discrimination.

What he didn't understand was that there had not been any discrimination because I had been there with her to support her! If I hadn't been there to fill the gap, she would never have coped.

Tiahna was effectively being penalised for doing well. She was being punished for being fortunate enough to have had parents who understood deafness who had given her the right communication for her from a young age.

The judgment implied that deaf children had to be doing very badly at school before they were entitled to Auslan support. We obviously had to wait until the system had failed them before giving them the access they needed. Tiahna had only succeeded at school because she had had support in Auslan through me. Now the judge had decided that she did not need Auslan because she was succeeding at school and could be educated in English. It made no sense!

What about Tiahna's educational future? Tiahna hadn't suffered, but I had. I had quit my job. Our family had put our lives on hold for five years, all for nothing. Five wasted years. The impact on my family had been immeasurable. I left court that day speechless, too upset to talk to anyone.

Meanwhile, Sam's positive court outcome meant significant consequences for deaf children in Queensland and throughout Australia. 'If any educational authority does not provide a deaf child with an interpreter when they need one, they would be in breach of federal human rights legislation,' said our counsel to the media. 'State Governments are now liable to pay compensation.'

But for Sam's family it was too late. No longer wanting to wait for Queensland to provide Auslan interpreters, they were forced to make the gut-wrenching decision to send Sam away to a specialist school for the deaf in Sydney, where he now lived with a host family. The family were devastated that their child was living away from home, but he was happier at the Sydney school because all his classmates could sign in Auslan. He was to spend the next two years there, separated from his family. The family said that they were unsure if Sam, now 12 years old, would ever recover from 'such a major educational setback'. (Since then, the whole family have moved to Perth and then back to Sydney, seeking a suitable school to meet Sam's needs.)

Following the judgment, the Queensland Education Minister, Anna Bligh, released a statement saying that 'over the past three years, [the] Department has substantially expanded support for the hearing impaired including the increased availability of Auslan sign language. Today's court decision supports the Department's current approach to education for the hearing impaired.'

On the same day the judgment was handed down, Deaf Children Australia (DCA) released a press release stating: 'It is our aim, and those of families, that all deaf and hearing impaired children are given the support to access education depending on their individual need – whether by sign language interpreter, notetaker or visiting teacher. DCA would like to see an educational system whereby all deaf and hearing impaired children, no matter what their hearing loss or support need, can achieve the same as their hearing peers.'

Bitter tears flow for loss of family

UPSET: Tiahna Hurst's plight is taking its toll.

AT every moment of cruel reflection Coolum mother Gail Smith burns into tears at the "injustice" of her family's situation.

Next month she and husband Jeff Hurst are uprooting siblings Tiahna, 7, and Jacobi, 3, and spending almost $10,000 on relocating to Western Australian so her profoundly deaf daughter can receive a higher level of learning support.

And Tiahna is also upset.

Yesterday the tension of recent weeks welled up along with the grief of seeing some of her things sold off in a garage sale to help lighten the family load.

These days she is not a happy girl at all.

And Tiahna's upset is another dagger in the heart of Gail as they prepare to pack with no jobs and no residence to go to at this stage.

The parents also have the prospect of paying court costs of a failed discrimination court case against Queensland Education hovering over their heads.

If the court orders they pay up, Gail estimates the bill would be somewhere between $150,000 and $250,000.

"If that happens I won't be paying one cent of it — I would rather go to jail," the defiant mother said as her fight to have her daughter taught Auslan sign language became increasingly desperate.

"It's time to move on — our family life has been on hold for five years."

Gail has decided it is worth taking the family across a continent where the education authorities there will provide Tiahna a full time interpreter as well as a teacher of the deaf and speech therapy.

In Coolum to lend the family a hand on the weekend was Gail's mother in law Jocelyn

HEART BREAKING: Tiahna Hurst, despite the pleading of mum Gail Smith, refused to pose for the story about she and her family moving to Perth for learning support.
Photo: Brett Wortman

Hurst, who ended up needing a shoulder to cry on as well.

"She was bursting into tears about every 10 minutes," Gail said.

"I cry every time I think about it as well."

Jocelyn said the tears have been a constant in her life since the court case, which Gail and Jeff intend to appeal with the help of Queen's Counsel Julian Burnside.

"This is tearing the family apart," Jocelyn said.

Gail said she does not want to leave her family behind.

"We're doing it for the kids — as a parent you do anything you can for them."

The family withdrew Tiahna from the Coolum State School where she failed to get the assistance it requested for her special needs. Gail believed the department's attitude was discriminatory and launched legal action.

Article published in The Sunshine Coast Daily, *23 May 2005*

Forced to leave Queensland

The staff and students at Tiahna's new community school were fantastic. But my daughter was still not being given full-time Auslan and I was forced to interpret for her every day in the classroom. This was neither fair on her nor on me.

The only alternative, it seemed, was to move interstate. At that time, Perth had almost 40 deaf children in mainstream schools who had full-time Auslan interpreters in their classroom plus additional support from speech therapists and teachers of the deaf.

In May 2005, we moved to Perth. In WA, Tiahna would be given access to a full-time educational interpreter so that I would be able to return to work and not have to worry about how much she was missing in the classroom.

It was the most devastating decision, having to uproot our whole family and leave our home and family and friends purely so that our deaf daughter could get a proper education. I did not want to leave Coolum. At any minute I kept bursting into tears at the injustice of it all. It seemed that deaf children were being forced to leave the state because the State Government was refusing to give them an education that suited their needs.

Yet we had to do it for Tiahna.

Jeff quit his job. We sold many of our belongings and had to spend almost $10,000 on relocation costs. We uprooted Tiahna, who was now seven and in Grade 2 and Jacobi who was three. Tiahna was devastated.

We left the state with no jobs and no home to go to. What terrified us most was the prospect of having to pay courts costs, which we estimated would be between $150,000 and $250,000. If it was ruled that we'd have to pay, I wouldn't have forked out one cent of it. They could throw me in jail as far as I was concerned. This court case had almost torn our family apart.

After lodging our appeal against the decision with the help of a Queen's Counsel, we began our new life in Western Australia.

Perth was amazing; we were very happy there. Quinns Rock Primary School, just north of Perth City, had everything Tiahna needed and more. Despite being the first ever deaf child at the school, Tiahna received her own full-time Auslan interpreter and had speech therapy every week. And I felt comfortable with the principal. He was open-minded, easy to talk to and open to negotiation with regards to Tiahna's needs.

I was able to return to work for the first time in years and began managing a hairdressing salon, which I loved. However, within a few months of starting, the school begged me to interpret for a five-year-old deaf student who had just begun Prep at the school. They'd been unable to find an interpreter and were desperate. Initially I politely refused on the basis of loving my new job, but felt torn. If someone had knocked back interpreting for Tiahna, it would have upset me. My boss from the salon begged me not to go and offered me half the business. But morally it felt wrong to say no. So I left the salon and spent the next two years interpreting for the little girl at the school.

Court battle won!

On 28 July 2006, the full Federal Court reversed its decision, deciding instead that the lack of Auslan support had in effect been harmful to Tiahna, regardless of whether she had coped in the circumstances. Not having Auslan, they stated, could eventually be detrimental in the long term and damage her ability to achieve her potential.

On appeal, all three judges in the Higher Court ruled in favour of our case, meaning that Tiahna was now entitled to receive a full-time Auslan interpreter at whichever school she attended in Australia. This included Education Queensland if we returned to Queensland, who were also now obliged to pay our legal costs.

It was the strangest feeling. After six years of hell, we had won the battle. We decided to move home to Coolum because being away from our family was tearing us apart. We are now happily living back in Queensland.

Queensland's change to Auslan

In July 2007, the Queensland Government announced that they were committing $30 million to implement Auslan into Queensland schools over the next four years. This meant a policy change to enable Auslan rather than Signed English to be used as the sign language of instruction for deaf and hard of hearing students.

There is no doubt that our cases caused the policy change. It would not have happened for another ten years if we had not fought for our rights to a quality education. Our cases brought to light the needs of deaf children in education and provided Australia with a new understanding of the relationship between deafness and language.

'Our cases brought to light the needs of deaf children in education and provided Australia with a new understanding of the relationship between deafness and language.'

Finally, deaf education in Queensland is being brought into line with international best practice and will likely result in a more effective education system for those children who rely on sign language.

I now sit on a reference group with the Education Department as a parent and as an Auslan advisor, engaging in discussions as to what to do with funds allocated to Auslan in schools in our district. I am thrilled that we have been able to put the past behind us and are now working together to provide a better future for deaf children in Queensland.

No regrets

The past six years were a constant struggle for our family, yet the battle was definitely worth it. I don't regret those years of fighting, because we got the result that we wanted for Tiahna.

I would have regretted it more if I'd had to go to school with Tiahna every day for her whole schooling because she didn't have an Auslan intepreter. I would have regretted looking at Tiahna when she was older, thinking, 'I should have fought for her more because look at how much she is suffering now.'

Tiahna is now ten and in Year 5 at a local primary school. With her full-time Auslan interpreter, she is going from strength to strength. People who have just met us often ask why I am

Tiahna with her dog Bailey

'using my hands with Tiahna' when speaking to her. When I tell them that she is deaf, they are taken aback. They tell me they hadn't noticed because she has such excellent speech. In her national benchmark tests, she is above average in writing for her year level. This is only because she has been given the right beginning. I can now rest easy in the knowledge that Tiahna is getting the right education which will set her up to do well in her life.

Reflections on parenting a deaf child

Please note that these are only my opinions and I respect the rights of parents to make their own decisions. I believe the following to be true:

• Deaf children can achieve exactly the same as hearing children, if given the right opportunities.

• Hearing children pick things up just by being in the same room, but deaf kids don't. If your child has just been diagnosed with deafness, start doing everything visually through gestures and one on one with them. Try and learn as much basic sign language as you can. Once your child has developed language, you can drop the signs.

We signed everything for Tiahna. When we went shopping, we would sit her in the trolley, the perfect place for face-to-face interaction. We would go through the fruit section and I would sign and say in a loud voice, 'I need three apples. One green apple in the bag. Two green apples in the bag...' People would walk past and think I was nuts, but I didn't care! This is what Tiahna needed and it became part of our routine.

With Tiahna, we'd show her an object or a picture of an object, then show her the sign, then we'd mouth the word to her without making a sound, then we'd say the sound without showing her the sign.

Every night, we'd read her a book. First, I'd sign the whole book to her in Auslan while she sat opposite me on the bed. The following night, I'd sit her on my lap so she couldn't see me. I'd reread the book to her, talking directly into her microphone at the back of her hearing aid so she'd have to listen. The third night, I'd sit her opposite me and read the same story. This time I'd mouth the words without changing my lip patterns. I would not make a sound so that she would learn to lipread. The fourth night, I'd sign the same story to her and tell her to tell me the story. Of course, by this time, she knew the story backwards. I believe this is why her language skills are so good.

• I would recommend that you provide your deaf child with access to both sign language and verbal language from a young age rather than waiting until they are older to learn to sign. In my experience, this leads to better adjusted, happier adults.

I have copped flack from the Deaf signing community because my child wears hearing aids and attended speech therapy. I have also copped flack from the auditory verbal centres and the cochlear community because my daughter signs. We were not allowed to access the free speech therapy offered by the auditory verbal centres because Tiahna signed. Even so I gave Tiahna both so that she could choose what worked for her and could fit into both worlds. Do not deprive your child of hearing aids or sign language.

- The way you react to your child's deafness is critical to their future happiness. Many parents' sad reactions to their child's deafness cause confusion in their child. When they grow up, they are not proud of who they are. I've taught my daughter to be proudly deaf. She loves her hearing aids because they give her sound. And she is not afraid to sign in public.

When she was five, she said, 'Mum, I'm deaf. Everyone's hearing and I don't want to be deaf.'

I said, 'I know, darling, that's just the way you were born. Everyone's different. If everyone was the same, the world would be such a boring place! Sometimes I wish I were deaf.'

'Why?' she said, shocked.

'Because then I wouldn't have to listen to the thunder at night, the cars revving up and down the street, people fighting or gossip.'

She now thinks deafness is 'cool'. Her little brother Jacobi, who is hearing, but bilingual, tries on Tiahna's hearing aids and says, 'It's not fair. I want hearing aids too, Mum!'

- Teach your child to stand up for themselves if they are being bullied. There was a situation when there were kids on the bus laughing and pointing at Tiahna's hearing aids. Tiahna turned around and said to them, 'Yeah, so what! I was born deaf, but you were born ugly and you can't fix that! At least, I can get a hearing aid!' It may not be politically correct and I would normally not encourage this type of response, but it worked for Tiahna. It's rare these days that she gets picked on. Most of the time, her classmates fight over who gets to be her partner because they can practise their sign language!

- Parents need to teach their child to advocate on their own behalf when they are old enough. Rather than you having to keep going into school and saying, 'My child can't hear that video and it has no captioning. Can you please get captioning or can I take it home and explain to her in Auslan?', encourage your child to do it for themselves.

Tiahna used to come home and say, 'Mum, I don't like my interpreter sitting so close to me! She's breathing down my neck and every time I am writing and not looking at her, she taps my desk really loudly so that everyone looks at me.'

I said to her, 'If I go in and talk to the interpreter, she's going to think I'm interfering. Tiahna, you are now 10. If you don't like something, tell her what you want. Tell her nicely that she is sitting a bit too close. Ask her to move back a bit. Tell her if she wants your attention to please tap you on the foot under the table rather than banging on the desk.' Tiahna now does this all the time and feels empowered that she is getting what she wants.

• Be sensitive to background noises. Deaf children switch off if they can't hear so try to eliminate or be aware of background noises like lawn mowers and radios.

• Deaf children only demonstrate behavioural problems when they become unable to follow what is going on.

• Take your child to deaf events so they can socialise with people like them and be part of a deaf world. Tiahna loves being around deaf people because they are similar to her.

9

My aim in life is to be happy with myself and I am!

With two bachelor degrees and a postgraduate degree, 30-year-old Lizzie Eakin (severe to profoundly deaf) has spent the last nine years working as an early childhood special educator – a career she is passionate about. She currently works in Sydney's south-west with families of children with a wide range of disabilities. Her hobbies include travelling, funk dancing, netball, socialising and hanging out with her boyfriend whom she adores.

I'VE NEVER SEEN MYSELF as 'different' to anyone else and because of that, people don't really treat me as such. They seem to like and accept me for who I am.

Mum and Dad believe that I was hearing when I was born because I slept in a bedroom near the front door and wouldn't go to sleep until Dad came home from work. At six weeks old, I contracted a viral ear infection which they believe is the cause of my hearing impairment. My hearing loss was progressive rather than an overnight thing.

It wasn't until I was 15 months old that Mum and Dad began to notice that something was really wrong because I stopped

155

responding to people calling my name. They spoke to my grandpa who was a doctor. He said, 'Yeah, there's something going on here,' and he referred me to an audiologist. I was diagnosed as having moderate to severe sensorineural hearing loss in both ears. By the time I was seven, this had progressed to severe to profound bilateral sensorineural hearing loss.

The most distressing thing was that the audiologist told my already upset mum that I would be scared of the dark, that I would never go to a normal school, that I wouldn't be able to make friends and a whole range of other negative untruths. She took Mum to another room where there was an older girl who had a similar hearing loss as I had. The girl couldn't speak very well, she had a great deal of trouble forming her words and she spoke with high pitched tones. The audiologist told Mum that that was how I would turn out.

From that moment on, Mum was determined that that was never going to be the case. She did a lot of research into hearing loss, she read books, asked heaps of questions and applied everything she'd learned. When she heard that kids who are hearing impaired have challenges with language development, she took me to the library and read stories to me all the time to help me develop my language. Mum did the bulk of work with me as Dad was busy working long hours and often travelled overseas for business.

I had an older sister and a brother 18 months younger, both of whom are hearing. Mum and Dad tried never to treat me any differently to them. As a child, I think Mum spent a lot more time with me than she did with them. My little brother would get dragged along to all the intervention programs I had to go to. I've asked my brother and sister, 'Have there ever been times in your life when you have felt affected by my deafness?' They both say no. My sister says she never felt that I was different, nor did she feel left out or anything. I don't know if she's saying that to be nice, but I don't think so. I think that they both just accepted me for who I was and realised that I just needed that little bit more help.

My first day of school!

I was fitted with two hearing aids when I was 18 months old that I still wear. I can hear quite a lot with them and I've been trained to use the 2% residual hearing I've got with the hearing aids. Without them, I can't hear anything at all. I'm in two minds about having a cochlear implant. Mum and Dad were given the option when I was younger, but they made the decision not to go ahead because cochlear implants were still very experimental at that time. They wanted to give my residual hearing a chance. Cochlear implants destroy any leftover hearing you have.

I've got three friends who are hearing impaired. One recently got an implant and the other is considering getting one too. Both have moderate hearing loss, but their speech is not as good as mine. I'm not sure why – maybe because of their parents' involvement? One got the cochlear implant a year ago at the age of 32. He says he's picking up a lot of sounds, but I don't know if it would be worth it for me. Maybe when I get older and lose more of my hearing and if it becomes less invasive, I might consider it. Right now, I'm quite happy to wear the hearing aids.

I can hear most sounds, but not high-pitched noises, like screaming. I can hear music and I can hear someone singing, but I can't hear the words they are singing unless they are familiar to me. If I read the words to the song and learn them off by heart, then I can sing along to them. But I don't know what I can't hear because I don't know any better. You know what I mean?

For my early intervention, I went to the Catholic Centre for Hearing Impaired Children at Strathfield where I participated in their auditory oral program. I received support from this program through pre-school and school. My parents decided to send me to mainstream pre-school, primary and high school. I never learnt how to sign when I was younger because my parents wanted so much for me to speak verbally. At pre-school, I was the only one who was deaf in my class. We used to do a lot of singing. I would just pretend that I knew the words to the songs and follow everyone else's actions!

Mum was pretty fussy about which primary school she wanted me to go to. She chose a local Catholic school, St Joseph's, at Oyster Bay, because it was small – only two classes per grade and 14 classes all up. I was the only child with hearing impairment in the whole school. A girl with spina bifida enrolled at the same time as me. It was the first time that they had students with disabilities at the school. As inclusive practice was a new thing then, the principal was determined to give it a go.

I took to school pretty well. I started wearing an FM unit in Year 3 and I had an itinerant support teacher from the Special Education Department of the Catholic Education Office, who visited me once a week. She used to take me out of class or help me in class. She trained my teachers to not turn their backs on me or write on the blackboard while they were talking.

She trained them to make sure that they turned around to look at me when they spoke.

She told them not to stand in front of the window because it was hard to see their face in the light. They would either draw the blinds or make sure they were standing against a dark background. If we were sitting on the floor, I was made to sit at the front, directly opposite the teacher so I could read her lips. I was taught to lipread rather than listen whereas now they are teaching children to listen and not lipread at all because it's more practical for them in terms of listening to the radio and television etc.

I had friends from day one really. I got some teasing when I was in Year 4. They called me 'deafhead', but I think that was just kids being kids really. I didn't understand what the comment really meant or the insult behind it. When I went home and told Mum – just in conversation really, not to get anyone into trouble or anything – she was very upset about it. Mum and Dad went to the school the next day and had a meeting with the principal and she called the boys into the office and made them apologise to me. I was like, 'Yeah, okay!' I didn't know what all the fuss was about!

I used to get so tired from concentrating so much during the day that I would fall asleep in the car on the way home or at the dinner table. We always had dinner at the table, I think because Mum wanted me to learn how to have a conversation with a number of people at the same time.

I went to St Patrick's High School with a lot of the same kids from my primary school so that worked really well for me. I was able to maintain some of the friends I'd had at primary and also make some new ones. I remember being petrified about starting high school, only because I was worried about how I'd do in exams and difficult subjects.

I was the only deaf person at my school for a while. Later on in the year, another girl started in the year above me, but she was only slightly deaf in one ear, so it wasn't really an issue for her. I had an itinerant support teacher again and the FM unit for a little while but I stopped wearing it at the end of Year 7 because it was such a pain taking it off the teacher and giving it to the next teacher at the end of each period. All it did was amplify the sound for me anyway. It didn't really make that much of a difference because I was more of a lipreader.

I always sat in front of the class so I already had the strategies to cope with the classroom situation without needing the FM. The rotary club gave me a laptop because the idea was for me to learn how to touch-type so I could look at the teacher and type. That didn't work either because I didn't have a printer so I couldn't print out my notes! So I just wrote in a book really.

Swapping from one teacher to another at high school was a bit of a challenge, probably because when I started, a lot of the teachers weren't aware that they were going to have a student with a hearing impairment. They kept forgetting so I'd have to keep reminding them! After a while, they began to remember who I was.

I didn't get teased at high school. I guess I was really lucky. I must have been doing something right – I don't know! I think my attitude had a lot to do with it: I just showed people that I was no different from them. I simply needed a little more help.

I was comfortable with my deafness. I even had friends who were willing to help me at school. In Year 8, the principal decided that I needed a buddy for each class, like a friend to help me, someone who I could ask questions to just in case I didn't hear the teacher. The principal decided that my buddy would change every school term. I remember the girls used to fight over who was going to be my peer buddy! I was so lucky!

I had teachers who were willing to help me in every way they could. Even when I participated in extra-curricular activities such as swimming, netball and athletics, the teachers and kids ensured that I always had ways to 'hear'. For example, at swimming when the hooter went off to start a race, someone would always be on the side, waving to me, to let me know when to go.

I always knew I wanted to work with children. I've always loved children and animals and I've always been interested in behaviour without words, if that makes sense. After finishing my Higher School Certificate, I went to university and completed two bachelor degrees and a postgraduate degree. For my first degree, I went to the University of Wollongong and did a Bachelor of Early Childhood Teaching for three years.

After that, I did a two-year Special Education degree by correspondence through Flinders University in Adelaide.

At my graduation from Flinders University

When that was over, I completed a Religious Education degree at the Australian Catholic University for three years. All up, I studied for eight years! I worked part-time in childcare while I was doing my Special Ed degree.

I had a notetaker at uni. That was good. It wasn't really much of an issue for me, because most of the time, the lecturers had notes on the overheads or gave Powerpoint presentations. Having a notetaker was a great reason not to attend the lectures because if I skipped them, I always knew I could go and get the notes off the notetaker!

Yes, I've had challenges and I've had to work hard at what I do, but only because I wanted to. It wasn't that I thought, 'I'm deaf so I've got to prove to people I can do it.' It was more, 'This is where I want to be so that's why I'm going to work hard'. I wanted to do it for me. The same motivation as everyone else really. I don't think I've had to work harder than anyone else to get to where I am.

I've spent the last nine years of life establishing a career as an early childhood special educator. My first special ed job was a one-year placement at the Department of Education Public School. It was called a School for Specific Purposes, basically meaning a school for children with special needs. I had a Year 2 class of six boys. Five of them had autism and one had cerebral palsy.

After that, I worked for two and a half years in an early intervention pre-school program for a disability service and also part-time in a primary school program. Now I work at an organisation called Learning Links, which is an early childhood intervention service in south-west Sydney. I run playgroups for children who have a wide range of special needs. I also consult with families, pre-schools and childcare centres.

I've never gone out with the attitude: 'I've got a disability and I'm going to show these families what their children are capable of.' My whole thing was I wanted to work with children and I was very drawn to children with disabilities because I could see that they were people, not disabled children. I'm very maternal and I care about people a lot.

I've found that there's a huge amount of respect from families I work with and I've had a few remarks that I'm an inspiration to these families because of the challenges I've had to overcome. This has given them hope for their children with additional needs, that they may achieve similar things.

Last year I had a mum say to me that because of me and my disability, she had hope for her daughter and that I was an inspiration to her. Her daughter has Down Syndrome, which is so much more than what I've got. I was really touched by that. It made me feel, 'Wow! I never thought that families would be thinking that way about me!' I was just thinking that they were looking at me as a specialist for children with disabilities, so that was a real eye opener.

Dad, Mum and me

I didn't have any deaf role models around me growing up, no deaf influences whatsoever. I never searched for any deaf role models because like I said, I never saw myself as someone who was different. Mum has always been my greatest role model and influence in my life. Mum and Dad integrated me into a hearing community so much that I never felt that I needed to be part of the Deaf community.

There were times during my teens when my hearing impaired friends tried to get me involved in the Deaf community. I would go along with them to the Deaf community get-togethers and parties, but I never felt like I fitted in. It wasn't just that I couldn't sign. It was the lifestyle they had. I felt that their whole lives were about being deaf. I saw no difference between being 'hearing impaired' and being 'deaf', but to them the difference was huge!

I was confused and used to ask them, 'What's the difference?' They would reply that I was 'hearing impaired' and they were 'deaf'. The feedback I was getting was that I didn't fit into their group.

I guess my attitude was different to theirs. I used to say I was 'deaf' until my experience with the Deaf community. Then I started to say I was 'hearing impaired'. Now I simply alternate between the two, whatever is quicker to say!

Left to right: Me, Leanne Ortika, Vicki Cowan (with black strapless top), Kath Behn (with flower necklace), Olivia Demir (in dress ups!), Emma Butler and Jo Johnson

I've got more hearing friends than I have deaf friends. I've only got three friends who are deaf or hearing impaired and I'm quite close to them but I worry about mixing my hearing friends with my hearing impaired friends. I know they talk a bit differently from me and they need a little more help than I do to understand hearing people. We all have different approaches and attitudes to how we handle our own disabilities.

I know someone who thinks the world owes her something for having a disability. She feels like she doesn't have to put in the hard work to get the rewards. She thinks that people should just give her a job and she's finding it difficult to hold one down because of this attitude.

I think her mum has a lot to do with this. Her mum's attitude towards her deafness is: 'If you have a disability, the world owes you!' I hate that because I don't think anyone owes you anything. If you are deaf, that's just the way you are and it's what you make of it. Sometimes though, I can understand that there will be circumstances where your disability can hold you back from getting a job so getting the pension isn't an issue in cases such as these.

When I finished my teaching degree I applied for a job with the Department of Education. I tried to get on the waiting list for a permanent job but they refused because I had a hearing impairment. I was quite upset and thought, 'If I had known that from the start, I would never have done a teaching degree.' If I'd been a hearing person, I would never have had that issue. I would simply have been put on the permanent list.

They sent me off for a medical assessment and the doctor checked my urine, my joints, my weight, my eye-sight and just about everything else, but he didn't check my hearing. I couldn't understand what the Department was trying to achieve. Then the doctor wrote a report stating what support I would require in the classroom in order to teach. The report said I would need another teacher to supervise me all the time, that I would need lots of light in the room to see and all this other rubbish that you couldn't possibly imagine.

I was so hurt. I felt like they hadn't even given me a chance. So I rang the Department of Education and asked to speak to the lady in charge. She refused to speak to me so I ended up getting legal advice and was going to take them to the discrimination court. It just took over my life. In the end I decided it wasn't worth it.

I decided to try something else. That's how I ended up in childcare and in early childhood intervention, which has worked out to be better for me anyway. Everything always falls into place.

I tried the school thing and had to fight for a one-year placement at the School for Specific Purposes. I had to have another interview though just to make sure that I was 'okay' and fit to teach, basically. I had to show them programs and work samples to show them how I would teach the kids!

I've only been signing for about nine years really. As I said, Mum and Dad were determined that I wouldn't sign when I was

'The most important advice I would give to parents of hearing impaired kids is to have a positive attitude, to encourage your kids and tell them that they can do anything!'

younger. It wasn't until I started working with children with disabilities that I began learning sign language.

In the work I do, I encourage what's called the 'Total Communication approach', which is a combination of signing and speaking as well as the use of pictures in order to communicate. My challenges growing up were mostly about missing out on things like music and conversations around the dinner table. I try to minimise this problem for the kids with complex disabilities I work with.

In this day and age, with a better understanding of hearing impairment and the introduction of cochlear implants, I believe that there is no reason why children with hearing impairment can't develop their speech.

I remember feeling constantly frustrated by my lack of language and vocabulary when I was younger. Quite often I'd get into trouble for things I didn't do and I didn't have the words to explain that I didn't do it or how it happened. I remember when I was six years old, I walked past a friend of mine in kinder and gave her a friendly pat on the hair. It was just a little pat. She burst into tears and said that I had hurt her. The teacher told me off and I couldn't tell her that I had simply meant to give her a friendly pat. The teacher rang Mum. Mum was angry and I didn't have the language to explain that I had never meant any harm and that it hadn't been intentional!

I would recommend to parents of hearing impaired children that they take the time to help their child find the right words, that they ask questions and try to see it from their child's side. I know this would be hard sometimes because you're angry and you want your child to do the right thing. Sometimes things are not what they seem; your child may have done nothing wrong.

I live in Cronulla with my parents. I haven't had the money to move out because I've been travelling on and off for the past seven years, but I'm saving! Travel has really opened my eyes. I've learned so much about different cultures, and about learning to be independent and making sure I have enough money to pay for dinner for the next week! I've backpacked overseas a number of times on my own and it has always been a very empowering experience.

The first time I went overseas, when I told my mum I was going, she tried every excuse in the book to stop me. I think she was really scared that something would happen to me. Like, if a smoke or a fire alarm went off in a hotel room no one would alert me to it and I'd be left behind. But I have never had a situation like that.

With today's technology, I don't feel like I miss out on too much. Mobile phones with the SMS feature and emails are a godsend. I don't know what I'd do without them! I think Australia could do more in terms of technological support for people with disabilities in general though, not just for people with hearing impairment. America is one step ahead of Australia with the technological support they provide people with disabilities. In comparison, our resources are fairly limited.

Living it up in Vienna, 2005

I look forward to the day Australia gets captions for all movies in every cinema so deaf people have the freedom to go to any movie they want. Right now, I have to travel into the city where they show the same movie three times a week with captions and another one the following week. There should be more captioning for TV shows, including *Music TV* or *Rage*. I can hear music; I just can't hear what the words are. It would be nice to sing the words!

I'd love to be able to connect a mobile phone to a TTY, like a portable TTY. You can do that over in the States and you can make TTY calls from mobile phones, but you can't do that here. In the States, you can also SMS the National Relay Service to ring someone up. Quite often, if I'm running late for an appointment and I'm driving, I can't let the other person know. I just have to run late and then apologise when I get there.

It would be nice if cochlear implants were a lot smaller than they are now and sat behind your ear rather than on your head. Australians should have more financial assistance from the government. Why should it end when you turn 21? I really struggled two years ago when my hearing aids broke and I had to pay $8000 for my new ones. I was lucky because I was still living at home and had no debts except for my car. I was able to get a loan. But what if I'd been married and had children and a mortgage? There's no way I would have been able to afford that!

What about people who simply don't have that kind of money? They have to miss out on hearing, not fitting into social situations, and not being able to work effectively. It makes me angry. Hearing aids have a lifespan between four and eight years so this will happen again and again throughout my life. I'm not demanding that they are free, just that there is some sort of subsidy.

Driving was a bit of a battle with my parents, although I'm sure it's like that for all young people when they start driving. My parents didn't use hand signals because they wanted me to try to hear. They'd yell out things like 'Brake!', 'Stop!', 'Go left!' 'Right!' I found it extremely hard to hear what they were saying.

Now, when there are people in the car, I get them to show me with their hands where they want me to go. Before they get in the car, I teach them some basic hand signals like 'Stop', 'Slow down', 'Speed up' or 'Pull over'. I don't know how other deaf people have coped with getting their licences, but with my mum and dad, it was hard.

See, Mum and Dad put a bit of pressure on me to try to hear, I'm sure for all the right reasons. I think they were just trying to get me to be as 'normal' as possible. They tried to make me hear on the phone so that I could use it just like everyone else and not have to use technology for the hard of hearing to make phone calls. But it just didn't work. I couldn't hear! Eventually, I got my TTY when I was 19, a lot later than everyone else.

My current workplace has been very supportive of my challenges. When I first started working there, they rang JobAccess and got advice as to how they could best support me. We had someone come out with equipment that would help me do my job effectively. I've got a TTY for my desk to make phone calls and a portable TTY because I make a lot of house visits.

I've also got a work mobile phone so I can do a lot of SMSing with colleagues and clients. I've got a computer with email and a vibrating pager so I know if someone rings our office doorbell. They even fitted strobe lights for the smoke alarm.

I've had four jobs in early childhood and disability settings prior to this one, but this is the first time a workplace has been so supportive. It has made a huge difference to the quality of my work. Their emotional support has been absolutely fantastic too. They always forget I have a hearing loss, which I guess is a compliment to me!

I find it very difficult when I'm sitting with friends in a noisy bar or restaurant. At times, I feel left out and tend to withdraw. But I try not to take it personally and will do my best to be sociable. I quite often end up having one-on-one conversations with the person sitting next to me or across the table. Or I just sit back and enjoy what's going on around me. I like 'people watching'. There's a lot to learn about a person from their body language.

When I meet new people, they are often curious about my deafness and want to know more about it. I try to talk about my hearing loss in a light-hearted, humorous way. I make jokes to make people feel more comfortable and less overwhelmed. Like once, I remember, in high school, someone shouted,

'What? I can't hear you!' and I said, 'Neither can I!' and they were shocked that I had made a joke about my deafness. I just laughed and they relaxed.

I do things like that because I want to show them that it's not a huge deal. I don't want people to look at me and think, 'She's deaf.' That is only *part* of who I am. There are so many more important facets to me than just my deafness! Because I've got the attitude that deafness isn't a big issue, people seem to accept me and like me for who I am.

I'm usually pretty good at coping with new people and the way they talk, but sometimes I have to say, 'Sorry I'm deaf. I can't understand you. I need you to slow down,' or 'I need to read your lips.' Yeah, I'm pretty confident about telling people that I'm deaf. My boyfriend is so over-confident about it, he tells people straight away and I'm like, 'Shhh!' I actually find it amusing!

At times, you know, hearing loss is an advantage. When I was younger, Mum would yell at me and I would simply walk out and pretend I hadn't heard! I live in a noisy neighbourhood so it's nice to be able to hear nothing when I'm trying to sleep. When I can't be bothered concentrating on what's being said during a meeting, I'll switch off mentally and can always make the excuse that I couldn't hear properly!

I've had a few boyfriends but Dave has been the best of them all. He accepts me totally for who I am and is very proud of me. He always makes sure that we get DVDs with subtitles and when we go to the movies he types messages on his phone to tell me what's happening! I'm like, 'Don't do that, you're going to miss out!' but he can't help it! He's got to make sure I know exactly what's going on. It's beautiful!

He always wants to be the one driving because he knows that when I drive, we can't have a conversation. He's really

Dave and Lizzie at
Sydney Harbour Bridge

good like that. His family is Italian. I've been very fortunate to be accepted by them because many of the Italian families I work with have a lot of difficulty coping with children with disabilities. Even his mum tells everyone that I'm deaf every time we go out to parties and things!

I currently do tap and funk dancing. Hearing the music has always been a challenge, but I've got a supportive teacher and fellow students who laugh with me at my mistakes. I play netball as well. I don't hear the high-pitched whistle, but I just use cues from others and when they stop, I know they've probably blown the whistle. I enjoy life like any other nearly-30-year-old does.

Every day I count my blessings that I have a large number of fantastic friends, a great social life, a supportive family and boyfriend. They know how passionate I am about equality and inclusion of children and adults with disabilities. They support me in every way they can. I want to get married and have kids one day. In the meantime, my aim in life is to be happy with myself – and I am!

Useful contacts

Organisations

Deaf Children Australia
Deaf Children Australia is a national not-for-profit organisation representing the needs of 16,000 deaf and hard of hearing children and their families across Australia.
Ph: 1800 645 916
TTY: +61 3 9510 7143
Fax: +61 3 9525 2595
Email: info@deafchildren.org.au
Webpage: www.deafchildren.org.au

Deaf Services Queensland
Provides a range of services to the deaf and hearing communities in Queensland.
Ph: (07) 3892 8500
TTY: (07) 3892 8501
Fax: (07) 3392 8511
Email: dsq@deafsq.org
Webpage: www.deafservicesqld.org.au

Parent Council for Deaf Education (PCDE)
Provides families of deaf and hard of hearing children in New South Wales with independent and unbiased information and support. Collaborates with parents, professionals, other organisations and government departments to promote equity of access to services and opportunities.
Ph: (02) 9871 3049
TTY: (02) 9871 3025
Fax: (02) 9871 3193
Email: pcde@bigpond.com
Webpage: www.pcde.org

WA Deaf Society
A non-profit organisation providing services to deaf and hard of hearing people in Western Australia.
Ph: (08) 9441 2677
TTY: (08) 9441 2655
Fax: (08) 9441 2616
Email: wadeaf@wadeaf.org.au
Webpage: www.wadeaf.org.au

Deafness Forum of Australia
Deafness Forum is the peak body for deafness in Australia.
Ph: (02) 6262 7808
TTY: (02) 6262 7809
Fax: (02) 6262 7810
Webpage: www.deafnessforum.org.au

Deaf Australia
Deaf Australia (formerly the Australian Association of the Deaf) is the national peak body managed by deaf people that represents, promotes, preserves and informs the development of the Australian Deaf community, its language and cultural heritage. It works towards a vision of an Australia where deaf people have no barriers.
Ph: (07) 3357 8266
TTY: (07) 3357 8277
Fax: (07) 3357 8377
Email: info@deafau.org.au
Webpage: www.deafau.org.au

Julie Phillips
Anti-Discrimination Consultant
PO Box 412
Fairfield VIC 3078
Ph/Fax: (03) 9481 0999
Mobile: 0417 570 197
Email: email2jphillips@yahoo.com.au

Hear For You
Hear For You is a mentoring program for young deaf people. It provides e-mentoring and group workshops aimed at helping young deaf people in mainstream schools to engage fully in life and realise their potential.
SMS +61 438 003 526
Fax: +61 2 8003 9759
E-mail: info@hearforyou.com.au
Webpage: www.hearforyou.com.au

Websites

www.deafchildrenaustralia.org.au
Resources, stories and online discussion groups for parents and deaf youth.

www.aussiedeafkids.org.au
Resources, stories and online discussion group for parents.

www.parentline.com.au
Another great parent support option.

www.deafchildworldwide.info
Ideas, discussions, research and information on all aspects of childhood deafness on a global scale.

www.ndcs.org.uk
The National Deaf Children's Society in the UK.

www.innovativeresources.org/default.aspx
Sells resources that might be useful for parents.

www.wom.com.au
Another site about latest technology.

www.signswap.com.au
Australia's most popular sign language reference.

www.hearingexchange.com
A good place to find information, communicate or comment on anything to do with deafness.

www.hearingdogs.asn.au
Soundfield systems for schools from Lions Hearing Dogs.

www.phonak.com/consumer/parents.htm
Practical hints and tips on hearing aids for parents, including the downloadable 'Oliver' books.

Other useful resources

Dictionary of Auslan
This is an English to Auslan dictionary featuring over 3000 signs, and is set out in a user-friendly A–Z format.
Price: $49.95

Dictionary of Auslan Images (CD-ROM)
This CD-ROM contains all the images from the new edition of the Dictionary of Auslan. Featuring over 3000 full-colour images of the signs, clearly demonstrated through photographs of people and arrows to show the movement of each sign.
Price: $60 for individuals/families, $90 for schools/organisations

Teach Yourself Auslan – Beginners
An innovative, self-paced learning tool aimed at beginner level Auslan users.
Price: $39.95

Beyond Ordinary: growing up deaf (DVD)
This DVD contains first-hand accounts of growing up deaf or hard of hearing in Australia.
Price: $15.00

All products can be ordered through www.deafchildrenaustralia.org.au

Glossary of terms

ABO blood incompatibility results when the blood type of the foetus differs from the blood type of the mother, for example, the mother is type O and the baby is either A, B or AB. When incompatibility occurs, the mother creates antibodies to defend against the blood type of her infant. These antibodies cross the placenta and begin destroying the baby's blood cells. The result is that the baby develops jaundice (yellow discolouration of the skin) which if untreated can create more significant problems.

Audiogram is a standard way of presenting a person's hearing loss. It is represented as a picture or a graph.

Auditory Brainstem Response (ABR) testing is a screening test to monitor for hearing loss or deafness, particularly in newborn infants. For this test, sounds are played to the baby's ears. Band-aid-like electrodes are placed on the baby's head to detect responses and can measure up to a 90 decibel loss.

Auslan (Australian sign language) is the preferred method of communicating among members of the Deaf community in Australia. It is the national sign language of Australia and is officially recognised as a separate language. It is a unique visual gestural language with its own grammar and ensures full and complete communication. The signing is not in English word order and is distinct from English. It allows deaf children to communicate from a young age, easily and completely with other people who know Auslan.

Bilateral versus unilateral hearing loss: Unilateral hearing loss is hearing loss in only one ear. This can cause great difficulty in hearing background noise and makes localising the source of a sound difficult. Bilateral hearing loss is hearing loss in both ears. In addition to hearing speech at reduced volume, bilateral sensorineural hearing losses can cause sounds to be distorted. Putting sounds together meaningfully can be a difficult task. Medical intervention is not usually possible and the loss is permanent. Hearing aids are frequently fitted to assist the child to hear, depending on the degree of hearing loss.

Bilingual means being able to use more than one language. Deaf children may struggle to learn English because they do not hear English well enough to become fluent. On the other hand, deaf children can learn Auslan naturally and easily if they are exposed to it. The Bilingual-Bicultural (BLBC) approach is an educational communication program for deaf children which uses Auslan. Acknowledging Auslan and English as two distinct languages, it instructs a child in Auslan as a first language to communicate with the Deaf community and other Auslan speakers and teaches English as a second language. The child learns English through reading and writing and their teacher explains to them in Auslan how English fits together – the sentence structures, vocabulary etc.

Cochlear implant (bionic ear) is a surgically implanted electronic device providing sound to a profoundly or severely deaf or hard of hearing person. People with mild or moderate sensorineural hearing loss are generally not candidates for cochlear implants. Unlike hearing aids, the cochlear implant does not amplify sound, but works by directly stimulating any functioning auditory nerves inside the cochlea with electric field stimulated through an electric impulse. External components of the cochlear implant include a microphone, speech processor and an RF transmitter. Similarly, an RF receiver is implanted beneath the skin. The transmitter has a piece of magnet by which it attaches to another magnet placed beside the receiver. When the receiver gets a signal, it transmits to the implanted electrodes in the cochlea. The speech processor allows an individual to adjust the sound level of sensitivity.

A cochlear implant will not cure deafness or hearing impairment, but is a prosthetic substitute for hearing. Some recipients find them very effective, others somewhat effective, and some feel overall worse off with the implant than without. For people already functional in spoken language who lose their hearing, cochlear implants can be a great help in restoring functional comprehension of speech, especially if they have only lost their hearing for a short time.

Cytomegalovirus (CMV) is a virus and a member of the herpes family that can be spread through coughing, contact with blood, urine or faeces, or via the mucous membranes such as those of the mouth and genitals. CMV can infect virtually any organ of the human body. If a foetus is exposed to the virus via the infected mother, it can cause hearing loss and/or mental retardation in the unborn child.

Deaf community: The Deaf community in Australia is a diverse cultural and linguistic minority group that encompasses a vast network of social, political, religious, artistic and sporting groups that use Auslan (Australian Sign Language) as their primary mode of communication. Accepting one's deafness as part of a person's identity is the core element in identification into the Deaf community who are often described as Deaf with a capital 'D' to emphasise their deaf identity; 'deaf' (with a small 'd') is used in this book to include all people who are deaf or hard of hearing. Identification with the Deaf community is a personal choice and it does not depend on one's degree of deafness, rather on identifying with the cultural model of deafness. Culturally Deaf people, whether they have hearing aids, cochlear implants or use sign language, view themselves not as disabled, but as a normal, linguistic minority group. Being proud of one's Deafness now takes full force in a variety of ways – such as the Deaf festivals that are fostered each year across Australia throughout the National Week of Deaf people.

Deafness and hearing loss: Deafness constitutes a hearing impairment or hearing loss in which a person's ability to detect or understand sounds is fully or partially decreased. People are classified as having different levels of hearing loss. These are: mild, moderate, severe and profound. 'Mild hearing loss' is defined as having hearing problems at around 26 to 40 decibels. People in this category may have difficulties keeping up with conversations, particularly in noisy conditions. 'Moderate hearing loss' classifies difficulty in hearing quiet sounds heard by people between 40 and 70 decibels. People in this category also have difficulty keeping up with conversations and find both a hearing aid and lipreading useful. 'Severe hearing loss' is encountered by people who find it difficult to hear at 70 to 95 decibels. People in this category will benefit from powerful hearing aids, but often they rely heavily on lipreading even when they are using hearing aids. Some also use sign language. 'Profound hearing loss' is defined as a hearing threshold greater than 90 decibels. People in this category are very hard of hearing and rely mostly on lipreading and/or sign language. The written word may be the only way that some of the people in this category can communicate.

There are two types of hearing loss: conductive and sensorineural. Conductive hearing loss is caused by problems in the outer or middle ear which prevent the sound from being 'conducted' to the inner ear and hearing nerves. The hearing may fluctuate and may affect one or both ears to varying degrees. Conductive problems generally affect the quantity (loudness only) of the sound that is heard. It is usually medically or surgically treatable. A common cause of conductive loss in children is middle ear infection.

Sensorineural hearing loss is due to a problem in the cochlea (the sensory part of the ear) or the hearing nerve (the neural part). It can be acquired or be present at birth. There is usually a loss of clarity as well as loudness, i.e. the quality and the quantity of the sound is affected. It is possible to have both a conductive and a sensorineural hearing loss. This type of loss is called a mixed hearing loss.

Early intervention centres aim to offer specialised support to all children with additional needs (in this case deafness) and their families, prior to school entry. Evidence has shown that support given to children from birth through to the early years of formal education has a significant effect on their development. Early intervention includes: identification of children and families who may require specialised support, building parents' skills in caring for their children with special needs, promoting the development of children across all areas, promoting independence and family ability to make informed decisions in all aspects and stages of intervention, and encouraging participation of all children in the local community.

FM units (radio aids, FM systems, microlinks) work in partnership with a hearing aid or cochlear implant. They are often given to children to use in school. The teacher wears the microphone and the child the transmitter. The FM is designed to help minimise background noise, allow the teacher's voice to be heard more clearly and the child to hear from a distance. Hearing aids by themselves have three major problems: firstly, they don't work very well over a distance; secondly, they amplify everything so background noise is a problem; and thirdly, reverberation can cause sound to be distorted. FM systems overcome all these problems so they may assist the deaf child in the classroom.

Glue ear is a colloquial term for Otitis media with effusion (OME), in which the middle ear becomes inflamed and filled with thick mucus. This may cause temporary hearing impairment, which can evolve into permanent impairment if there is erosion of the middle ear structures.

Grommets aid in alleviating the symptoms of glue blockage by relieving pressure on the ear and allowing fluid to drain back though the nasal passage. Once air can enter the middle ear it helps improve children's hearing by allowing the tiny bones of hearing to move freely again. The grommets will gradually fall out of the drum after three–eighteen months. Most children's hearing will fully recover. The fluid may come back in some children and further treatment will be needed.

Hearing aid is an instrument that amplifies sound to assist people with hearing loss. They are distinguished by where they are worn: in the ear (ITE), in the canal (ITC), completely in the canal (CIC), behind the ear (BTE), or on the body. The hearing aid microphone picks up the sound, makes it louder and then transmits the louder sound (or parts of the sound) down through the hearing aid mould into the ear. Hearing aids can be analogue or digital. Each suit the level of your child's hearing loss.

Hearing loop is a loop of wire installed around the perimeter of an area, such as a cinema or a church, and connected directly to an audio amplifier, to assist people with hearing loss.

Meniere's disease affects the inner ear, the seat of hearing and balance. It often causes the person to feel dizzy and sick, and their hearing is dominated by a loud roaring sound to the point where one or both ears feel ready to burst. This is deemed to be the cause of fluid inside the hearing and balance mechanism of the ear. However, treatment can be difficult as no one knows the cause. Treatment options can range from medication, lifestyle change, operations to drain the fluid and operations to cut the balance nerve.

National Relay Service (NRS) is an Australia-wide telephone access service provided for people who are deaf or have a hearing or speech impairment. NRS is available 24 hours a day, seven days a week, and provides access to anyone in the wider telephone network. When the deaf person calls someone via the NRS, a relay officer will assist with their call. The deaf person can type and read their conversation entirely via a TTY or a computer with a modem. In some cases, the relay officer becomes the deaf person's 'voice' and reads out loud their conversation to the other person. The relay officer then listens to the response and types it back for the deaf person to read. The National Relay Service may be contacted on 1800 555 630 (TTY), Tel: 1800 555 660 (voice), Fax: 1800 555 690 or Website: www.relayservice.com.au.

Oral method, aural/oral and Cued Speech: The oral methodology consists of three different approaches. In the auditory verbal method, the child is taught through intensive teaching to use their remaining hearing to learn to speak. No visual cues, such as lipreading, facial expressions or natural gestures are used. Emphasis is placed on the child's personal amplification system and/or cochlear implant.

The aural/oral method also aims to teach deaf children to speak and lipread, but this method accepts the use of lipreading and natural gestures. Children will use their hearing aids and/or cochlear implant.

Cued Speech is a system of hand movements near the mouth to assist lipreading. Many sounds look the same on the lips and Cued Speech is used to assist the deaf and hard of hearing child to distinguish between them. Children will also use their hearing aids and/or cochlear implant to aid communication. The aim of Cued Speech is to assist communication through speech and lipreading. Cued Speech is not a sign language and is very rarely used by deaf adults. It is generally used in educational settings only.

Signed English is a made-up, hand-expressed code for English, which is not used outside of educational settings. Unlike Auslan, it is not a separate language. It was introduced into the Australian education system in the 1970s to try and improve the literacy, communication and reading skills of deaf children. People speak and sign at the same time when Signed English is used. Deaf adults rarely use Signed English.

Soundfield amplification classroom: When a classroom is equipped with a soundfield amplification system, all the children, regardless of seat location and the direction the teacher is facing, are able to hear the teacher equally well. This also provides the teacher with an opportunity to maximise the listening and learning opportunities in a classroom. An amplification system includes a wireless microphone/transmitter that the teacher wears (similar to a FM unit), a receiver, an amplifier and 2–5 individual speakers or a single ceiling-mounted speaker. The teacher's voice is amplified and projected out into the classroom via the speakers. A variety of researchers have reported favourable findings of the use of soundfield amplification systems in a classroom. Studies have been done with various academic and pre-academic behaviours for both students with normal hearing and students with hearing losses. Results have found an increase in positive behaviour and/or achievement in academics because of the soundfield amplification system.

Stethoclip is like a stethoscope used by doctors but it has a piece of tubing which connects to the hearing aid, enabling a person to listen to the aid. It is important that your child hears as well as possible through their hearing aids at all times. Wearing a hearing aid when it is not working properly can be worse than not wearing the aid at all. As children grow older and more experienced with their hearing aids they can learn to detect problems themselves. However, until they are able to do this your child will rely on you to check their hearing aids for them. Ideally they should be checked every day. To check your child's hearing aids, you can obtain a stethoclip or a special earmould (ask your Australian Hearing audiologist how to obtain these).

Processor is part of a cochlear implant that converts speech sounds into electrical impulses to stimulate the auditory nerve.

RF unit (audio loop, radio frequency system): Some people with a hearing loss benefit from the use of a type of technology called an 'audio loop' or a 'radio frequency system'. This technology requires the speaker to wear a special microphone which does not amplify sound, but rather 'streams' it directly into the user's hearing aid with a great reduction in background noise. This means that the users can better focus on the speaker's voice to enhance their ability to pick up speech sounds. Most users of this technology have a moderately severe to severe hearing loss and generally rely completely on 'oral' communication (lipreading as well as listening).

TTY (teletypewriter or text telephone) is a mechanical object that resembles a small thick keyboard with an inbuilt display screen. Instead of talking and listening, messages are typed to another using the keyboard. When typing, the machine converts the keystrokes into electronic signals which are then transmitted via telephone lines. The conversation appears in text on the small display screen on the other person's TTY. Calls can be made to another TTY user or relayed by the National Relay Service (NRS) officers. TTY can be used by anyone, irrespective of their hearing status.

Visual communication is simply communication in the form of visual aids. It allows the conveyance of ideas and information in forms that can be read or looked upon. It relies entirely on sight and can include signs, typography, drawing, graphic design, illustration and colour.

Volume phone has an adjustable volume control which can make the person's voice on the other end of the telephone sound louder.

Sound advice can make all the difference

WHEN YOU FIRST DISCOVER that your child has a hearing loss, it is common to feel overwhelmed by the choices that have to be made as to how to best support your child's development. You may not be fully informed of all your options, feel pressured to adopt one communication approach over another or experience the stress of having to make rash decisions. At this point what is most important is your relationship with your developing child and to be able to respond to their needs.

The support of parents who have already been through these experiences can often be a source of great comfort and inspiration. Deaf Children Australia believes that family to family support is one of the best ways parents can gather the knowledge and skills they need to navigate the world of deafness. In addition to information, advocacy and support services, Deaf Children Australia assists parents to provide those important networks through parent support groups, mentoring programs and a parent helpline.

**For more information, support and referral,
please call the Deaf Children Australia Helpline
on 1800 645 916 (telephone & TTY).
Available Australia-wide, Monday to Friday
from 10am to 4pm (EST).
You can also email helpline@deafchildren.org.au
or visit www.deafchildrenaustralia.org.au.**

Deaf Children Australia's vision is:
A life to be lived – deaf people empowered,
connected and achieving.

What Deaf Children Australia provide:

- Unbiased, up-to-date information
- Advocacy
- Accommodation service
- Audiology
- Auslan tuition
- Community development
- Counselling and psychology
- Education support services
- Employment service
- Family services and skills training
- Interpreting services
- Language and communication
- Physiotherapy
- Speech pathology
- Recreation activities and camps

*Only through donations from people who care can we
continue our work in helping the deaf children of Australia.
If you would like to make a donation, please contact
1800 645 916 or visit www.deafchildrenaustralia.org.au.*

*Deaf Children Australia has been enriching the lives
of deaf and hard of hearing children and young
adults for the last 149 years.*

To order a copy of this book, please go to www.deafchildrenaustralia.org.au

Quick order form

Fax orders:	Please fax this form to +613 9525 2595.
Telephone orders:	Please call 1800 645 916 or +613 9539 5300. TTY: +613 9510 7143 Please have your credit card ready.
Email orders:	info@deafchildren.org.au
Postal orders:	Please mail this form to: PO Box 6466, St Kilda Road Central, Melbourne, Victoria 8008 Australia
Pick up a copy from:	Deaf Children Australia 597 St Kilda Road, Melbourne

☐ Please send me ☐ copies of the book.
Book costs $24.95 plus $5.00 postage and handling.

☐ Please put my name on the Deaf Children Australia mailing list so I may
receive FREE information about events, workshops and other services.

Name:

Postal address:

City: State: Postcode:

Telephone/TTY:

Email address:

Payment details *(please tick one)*

☐ Cheque – payable to Deaf Children Australia   ☐ Money Order

☐ Invoice (for organisations/schools only)

☐ Visa   ☐ MasterCard   ☐ Amex   Expiry ☐☐ / ☐☐

Card No. ☐☐☐☐ ☐☐☐☐ ☐☐☐☐ ☐☐☐☐

Name on card

Signature

**How did you find this book? Julie would love to hear your feedback or
your own story. Please email Julie at jpostance@deafchildren.org.au.**

CPSIA information can be obtained at www.ICGtesting.com
Printed in the USA
BVOW011157070713

325049BV00006B/45/P